LEARN THE SECRETS TO TAMING WILD IDEAS, SIGN-UP FOR OUR CREATIVITY PROGRAMME.

CULTURECODE
The virtual creativity school

www.culturecode.courses

The goal of the Pitcher Awards is to provide the true and authentic pan-African benchmark for creative excellence. Pitcher Awards is open to work created, released or implemented anywhere on the African continent. Winners of the fourth edition were announced on 22 May 2021 as part of the Pitcher Festival of Creativity, which took place from 19 – 22 May 2021. The entries were judged by 4 independent juries under the categories of Channel, Digital & Good, Entertainment and Heritage.

African entertainment profile is on the rise and we figured that to adequately capture the impact of this very important sector of business and development in the region, it was necessary to give it its own category. This led to the creation of the Entertainment category in 2021. The impact of COVID-19 on mankind has been monumental and we thought it would be great injustice to posterity if we did not capture the ideas that were birthed in the wake of the pandemic. This necessitated the creation of a special one-off subcategory for COVID-19 under the Pitcher for Good category. This subcategory honours great ideas that were developed to address the impacts of the pandemic.

As you will find in the pages that follow, despite the difficulty brought about by the COVID-19 pandemic, creativity never took the back seat in Africa. We are grateful to the jurors working from across Africa for the hard work and diligence they have put into curating these great ideas. Congratulations to all the winners.

Nnamdi Ndu
Chairman, Pitcher Festival of Creativity

Contents

Media Agency of the Year

Advertising Agency of the Year

Cover Credit: CIRCUS! Mauritius, Moka, Mauritius

MEET THE CHANNEL JURORS

PRESIDENT
AKUA OWUSU-NARTEY
Regional Managing Director
Ogilvy Africa

ARISTIDE MABATTO
Managing Director
ACMAR Media Group, Douala, Cameroon

GRAHAM DENEYS
Group Strategy Director
Carat, Cape Town, South Africa

DEMOLA SALAMI
Chief Operating Officer
BrandEye Media, Lagos Nigeria

STEPHEN ONAIVI
Managing Director
mediaReachOMD, Accra, Ghana

AUSTIN EFIENAMOKWU
Founder & CEO
Ubiquity Media Holdings, Lagos, Nigeria

TOKUNBOH GEORGE-TAYLOR
Managing Director
Hill+Knowlton Strategies, Lagos, Nigeria

Integrated Campaigns, Pr & Reputation Management, Use Of Data, Use Of Influencers Brand Ambassador
Use Of Insights And Strategy, Use Of Media

Integrated **Campaigns**

BRAND   Mauvilac Industries Ltd
ENTRANT COMPANY   CIRCUS! Mauritius, Moka, Mauritius
AWARD   Gold

Mauvilac ColourVogue 2020

Credits

Vincent Montocchio, CIRCUS!, Executive Creative Director

Sharon Gouges, CIRCUS!, Creative Director

Lara Marot, CIRCUS!, Client Service Director

Diana Botte, CIRCUS!, Client Service

Melissa Veerapen, CIRCUS!, Art Director

Julie Telot, CIRCUS!, Designer

Jean Christophe Ha Seng, CIRCUS!, Production Manager

Danitza Vithilingem, CIRCUS!, Producer

Kunal Jankee, Freelance, Videographer/Photographer

Background
Mauvilac, a local paint manufacturer in Mauritius, usually gives a full range of its latest and most trendy and sexy colours to the public though a catalogue called Colour Vogue.

Creative Idea
The problems with catalogues is that they are never really sexy or trendy. This year, our inspiration drove us towards an art installation using fashion and contemporary art to present the new colours. So we created a whole universe using only painting elements and tools.

Strategy
Lead like an art installation, the colours were integrated in the whole setup to bring the colours to life. Models and sets were presented in a novel and creative way to showcase the latest trends and colours. The artworks were then filmed and stills were used on various mediums which caught the eye of the public, as well as those of the top-notch influencers, architects and interior decorators to discover Mauvilac's new range of colours.

Execution
Brushes, pots, lids and reconverted paint samples were used throughout in a creative way to create an unforgettable art installation that is inspired fashion and contemporary art.

Results
The colours were brought to life through the painted bodies of the different models who were made to look like a living masterpiece in each room of the house.

BRAND   Sonatel Orange Group
ENTRANT COMPANY   Caractère, Dakar, Senegal
AWARD   Gold

JigeenJangal

Credits

Muriel Kla, Caractère, Executive Creative and Digital Director

Alexandre Julienne, Caractère, Artistic Director

Carole Bordes, Caractere, Copyriwter

Ernesto Hane, Caractere, Chief Innovation Officer

Ndeye Maguette Diawara, Caractere, Offline Project Manager

Mactar Diallo, Caractere, Social Media Manager

Ndeye Rokhaya Diop, Caractere, Online project Manager

Benedicte Samson, Caractere, Digital Factory Executive producer

Ousmane Fall, Challenger, Producer (Films)

Gregory Ohrel, Challenger, Director

seynabou Sarr, Caractere, Copywriter Junior

Aram Beye, Caractere, Community Manager

Ali Diouf, Caractere, Head of strategy

Moussa Boye, Caractere, Media Manager

JigeenJangal

Background

Sonatel Orange Group is the historical operator and leader in Senegal, also present in Mali, Guinea, Guinea Bissau and Sierra Leone. Although the group is very involved in the fields of education, the environment, culture and health through its foundation and its numerous CSR actions, its institutional image reflects its economic success rather than its societal commitment.

Creative Idea
Insight
Every year a girl stays at school, her future earnings increase between 10% to 20%.
In Senegal, girls outnumber boys and have better results at middle school.
But at the University girls make only 40% of total student population due to various social barriers.
Challenge
Commit to keeping girls in school and make Sonatel Orange the Herald of this issue.
Creative idea
Engaging the community through emotion (Film fiction "On the way to school – Format 2mn et 4mn) and sharing experience (Social Experience) broadcasted only on digital). A platform (HumanInsideAfrica.com) that highlights the commitments of Sonatel Group and especially that for keeping girls in school through testimonies and true stories. #JigeenJangal (Girl Learn)

Strategy
Our strategy with this campaign for the «Keeping girls in school» was to encourage it into a more engage Human centric discourse, to tell stories to start the conversation and mobilize in order to (re)position itself as a major player in Social Development.
Media strategy (off and online) : low expenses and a lot of effects. The campaign's offline media budget (tele-Radio-Press) is less than €40,000. In digital, the media budget is €0. 2 live talks with 5 influencers, who signed up for free, made the film viral and started the conversation. The first livetalk took place the day before the launch, with the film being shown in preview on a TV set where a representative of the brand to discuss with education specialists. The 2nd Livetalk took place on the day of the launch and triggered many conversations where the #JingeeJangal was widely used: 33 million impressions in less than 10 hours.

Execution
The launch of the campaign took place on the eve of World Education Day with a TV platform sponsored by the brand dedicated to girls' education in Senegal.

On this set the leaders of the group intervened.
The emotional film "On the Way to School" was premiered, launching the conversation around #JigeenJangale. On D-Day (February 24, «World Education Day») the film was broadcast on TV and social media with a call to action inviting people to visit the humaninsideafrica.com platform, listen to the podcasts and share their experiences as well. In radio, we also activated by broadcasting excerpts of podcasts testimonies inviting listeners to connect. On D+3 a series of stories were broadcast on Facebook and Instagram referring to the web platform. The conversation essentially focused on Twitter with an effective influence strategy. On D+8 we then activated the second part. That of the experience with the broadcast of the film «testimonials» on our online channels.

Result
A positive, activist and action-oriented digital conversation hailed by all for its relevance and the emotion it generated, the #JiggeenJangal campaign generated an impressive stream of spontaneous testimonies. Young girls, women, but also fathers, brothers, or fellow students told of the barriers, the stops, the injustices, the broken dreams or, on the contrary, the paths of hope and pride that they experienced or crossed. These numerous testimonies opened the way to a change of mentality but also to proposals, Relationships or supportive and inspiring initiatives such as bringing highly educated women into schools to talk to young girls about trades and guidance, etc. The Jigeen Jangale campaign showed the Sonatel Orange group from a new perspective, sharing a unifying, modern and positive vision of society. Its willingness to accompany change with a strong voice was all the more perceived as it was legitimate in view of its long-standing support for girls' schooling, the digital inclusion of women and a gender-sensitive human resources policy. #JingeenJangal has federated speech and demonstrated that a societal and committed momentum can make things happen. As of March 30, 2020, the campaign reached more than 60% of the population in TV and radio and reached over :-6,200 mentions of the hashtag; -30,900 interactions; -132 Millions in digital of impressions.

BRAND Tolaram Group
ENTRANT COMPANY mediaReach OMD, Maryland, Lagos, Nigeria
AWARD Bronze

Hypo Disinfection Campaign

Credits

Emmanuel Adediran, mediaReach OMD, Lead Strategist

Jubilee Okuwe, mediaReach OMD, Media Buyer

Precious Adeleye, mediaReach OMD, Media Planner

Farouq Bakare, mediaReach OMD, media Buyer

Hypo Disinfection Campaign

Background
Hypo bleach is one of Nigeria's most successful brands, having dominated the bleach category with over 95% market share in less than 4 years after launch, the objective for this year was to grow by 50%. One of the challenges the brand faced is that consumers only relate to the whitening property of bleach and only use it for laundry of white fabrics. This meant the consumption occasion for bleach was limited to a few times a month. To drive growth, we would need to look at creative ways to increase usage occasions among consumers.

Creative Idea
COVID 19 presented the perfect opportunity to drive new association for the functions of bleach & brand Hypo. The WHO listed bleach as a disinfectant in its COVID 19 guideline (We know the populace relied almost entirely on trusted sources like the CDC and WHO for information about the virus and quickly adopted all recommendations). We figured we needed to leverage the situation to show bleach as more than a whitener but also as a potent yet affordable disinfectant. This gave birth to our new campaign Wipe off COVID with Hypo which later evolved to Wipe off Germs with Hypo

Strategy
The overall strategy was to drive the new brand message via a high impact re-launch campaign across multiple media touch points namely TV, Radio, OOH, Digital & BTL. To achieve this, we followed a 3 step approach of Tell, Show and Convert.

Execution
TV: We deployed heavy spots placements targeting News & other high affinity content (News, drama, and health) as well as segment sponsorship on live TV shows where we engaged the TG educating them on the new brand benefits. We had TV presenters visit the open markets every Thursday for a live demo with the activation team and broadcast on TV

Radio: served as a reminder medium and frequency driver with spots while we used on air hypes and OAPs to educate and engage TG

Campaign was launched on OOH via LEDs for quick impact and reach across major areas; we had presence within malls for TOMA at point of shopping. We also deployed over 90,000 flyers in 25 major markets across 12 cities and residential areas with our message. We activated in places of worship and also made donations to gov't parastatals like FAAN. On Digital asides display and video ads on top ranking sites and social media, we employed influencers to demonstrate use of hypo and emphasize its importance as a disinfectant.

Result
The campaign worked, post campaign survey, we reached over 100m Nigerians and our Ad recall was 90% exceeding that of other popular disinfectants like Dettol. From sales report, rather than a decline in a time when consumption could have declined, sales of Hypo for the campaign period increased by over 86% and revenue increased by 98%. We achieved 40% attribution for Hypo as a disinfectant in 3 months surpassing its whitening property. By showing the multiple benefit of the product, we were able to drive increase in consumption frequency (BHT report showed the average usage occasion increased Weekly from 26%-35%, Daily from 1% - 4% & less than 2x monthly reduced from 21-17%). This campaign made it easy for consumers to see, know and accept Hypo Bleach as more than a Fabric Whitener but also an affordable disinfectant.

https://drive.google.com/file/d/1ONDtyFRwzXnsjrkk8tw dbKgb0ZAE2fcj/view?usp=sharing.

BRAND Tecnicil Indústria
ENTRANT COMPANY Mantra Pu, Praia, Cape Verde
AWARD Bronze

Spirit Tonic Water

Credits

Júnior Lisboa, Mantra, Creative Director

Júnior Lisboa, Mantra, Planner

Júnior Lisboa, Mantra, Copywriter

Ariston Quadros, Art Director

Spirit Tonic Water

Background
We were challenged to launch a new product, a national tonic water brand that would compete with foreign brands with a long history, notoriety and market acceptance. With the need to launch new tonic water in the Cape Verdean market, another problem arrived: how to make an impactful launch when everything is closed due to covid-19?

That was the atmosphere around the launch of Spirit, but, aware of the importance of a new homemade national product with a differential as Spirit is, we knew we had to make a difference.

Creative Idea
As part of a mixing process, Spirit as tonic water is part of a ritualistic prep. As a mixer, you are always aware of the details to make the best drink you can. That was our motto. With the concept "Spirit, made with soul" we considered that a drink always used as part of an experience, Spirit is connected with something deeper: a need, a memory, a moment. Even more, when everything is closed, Spirit needed to be more linked with the roots of what makes us drink: to live and have a purpose. A moment to share. Being aware of that was important to a 360° campaign: from branding to the packaging, offline and digital.

Strategy
Everything started with the brand. Spirit, as the naming says, is about something in us. Something ethereal and elegant. From that, we needed to materialize. First, to launch the brand we made packaging with two cups, in order to empathize the importance of moments. We selected bar owners and relevant personalities in Cape Verde received our packaging: they grow exponentially the awareness of the product, but most important they laugh, they shared, they lived.

Execution
With the use of TV, Radio and social media, we engaged a big audience. With the opportunity to give a new look to the Tonic Water content, we focused on elegance and raised awareness to mocktails, due to the new Cape Verdean Non-alcohol advertisement law. With a contest where everyone could share their receipts with Spirit, we offer the last branded gifts to our community. In parallel, we offered, once the bars were opened, a 2 for 1 cocktail promo with Spirit, in order to make everyone share what is important: their souls.

Results
In the end, from the detail of a new brand to the branded gift, TV and Radio, and the Social Media and offline promo's, we were able to reach almost 20% of the Cape Verdean population. Even with Covid-19 restrictions and the advertisement restrictions we were aware of something that was able to make everything possible - even in 2021, you can have your moments.

Credits

Hugo Jorge, Copywriter

João Vaz, Mantra, Copywriter

André Ferraz ,Art Director

Mariana Laurência, Mantra, Art Director

Daniela Lesco, Mantra, Social Media

Xavier Lopes, Mantra, Digital Strategist

Mara Anjos, Mantra, Account Manager

Oneida Cruz, Mantra, Account

Catarina Pereira, Mantra, Operations

BRAND   Diageo Ghana
ENTRANT COMPANY   mediaReach OMD, Accra, Ghana
AWARD   Silver

House of Walker

Credits

Gideon Quaku, OMD, Team Lead

Toyinnade Bello, OMD, Planner

Frances Quarcoopome, Jam Jam, CEO

Taniya Mondal, OMD, Account Director

House of Walker

Background
As part of the 200th anniversary of the brand Johnny Walker in Ghana, it was very important to drive scale in market to show the equity that the brand is made of with a target to have consumers experience the brand like never before. The media objective was to create massive impact demonstrating creativity at its peak in a manner that will guarantee consumer engagement and conversations beyond the time of year.

Creative Idea
The idea was to create a 'Never Been Seen' experience for our consumers to emphasize the brand heritage globally and locally. The creative idea was to get a Johnnie Walker Pop Up Store that will bring to life the brand experience and heritage live in Ghana. We were going to creatively deliver impact by using both ATL channels & BTL in a way not done before in our market.

Strategy
The strategy was to use an interplay of ATL channels and experiential (BTL) to tell the brand story in a manner that captivates Ghanaians and gets them talking all through the campaign period and beyond.

We were deliberate to select online and offline media channels that will deliver on our impact objectives and seamlessly integrates with the BTL plans. For offline, OOH and TV were prioritized create impact, drive reach & awareness. While digital was deployed to extend reach and drive conversations among TA around the experience curated at the House of Walker center; we employed social media & influencer marketing to drive conversations and enhance WOM, programmatic buying ensured our targeting was optimal and extremely efficient.

For BTL : Our House of Walker was designed to create the memorable experiences that matched the anticipation we had built using other ATL media channels

Execution
The activation started with the deployment of empty boxes on the street to create suspense.

These boxes housed mega-sized statue of the Signature Johnie Walker figurine - "The Striding Man" but they were not unboxed until one week to the launch date.

The unboxing of the Striding Man statues across key locations in Accra created lots of conversations and was further amplified by our partner influencers. On the Launch day, there was TV takeover for two hours with live coverage of the event but done in a very stylish format with pre recorded content and Johnnie Walker story fused into the live coverage. It has been described as one of the smartest and best brand live coverage in Ghana. Two channels leveraged were TV3 to drive local connection and Trace to show the brand with a global media platform to deliver top notch quality content. Post the launch date, digital contents were deployed across social platforms & via programmatic.

Nothing like this has happened in Ghana before.

Results
We were the talk of Ghana all through the campaign. Campaign delivered 88%+ reach and recorded over 20m+ TV viewership on launch day. This resulted in an oversubscription of the limited edition bottles by over 60% over the period. We trended week on week and did achieve our objective of creating a memorable experience for our TA.

BRAND   Pitstop Lagos
ENTRANT COMPANY   Arden & Newton, Ikoyi, Lagos, Nigeria
AWARD   Silver

Equalize Pay Gap

Credits

Perez Tigidam, Arden & Newton, Creative Director

Lynda Nwaizu, Arden & Newton, Copywriter

Tayo Odugbesan, Arden & Newton, Creative editor

Tariah Iwoba, Arden & Newton, Account manager

Eze Wodu, Arden & Newton, Account Manager

Festus Iyorah, Arden & Newton, Communications Associate

Equalize Pay Gap

Background
Men earning more than their female counterpart is a social issue that happens in almost every country. While other countries have started making policies to revert this practice, Nigeria is still in denial that this problem exists.

The objective of the campaign was to start a much needed conversation around gender pay gap that exists in Nigeria.

Creative Idea
To start a conversation around this discrimination against women and in celebration of International Women's Day, Pitstop Lagos created an "unfair advantage" in order to equalize women for a weekend by making them pay less for their meals and drinks.

Strategy
The strategy was to trigger the much needed conversation by creating an "unfair advantage" for women.

Execution
We started the campaign by announcing the special discount for women. Next was the live event where we interviewed women on what they thought about the gender pay gap. Then the press release was released with data backing up the gender disparity in pay and finally, the case film was released.

Results
The content response was amazing as the much needed conversation was had on Twitter and Instagram.

BRAND   William Grant & Sons

ENTRANT COMPANY Mediafuse Dentsu - Vizeum, Ikeja, Lagos, Nigeria

AWARD   Bronze

Glenfiddich Where Next?

Credits

Joshua Oyeleye, Vizeum Media, Manager

Korede Ladejobi, Posterscope, OOH Asst. Manager

Olajumoke Ajayi, Vizeum, Media Executive

Nosa Ojo, Prodigy, Managing Director

Micheal Ogundimu, Prodigy, Media Works Services

Radley Connor, William Grant & Sons South Africa (Pty) Ltd, Senior Regional Marketing Manager

Lauren Kritzinger, William Grant & Sons South Africa (Pty) Ltd, Head of Marketing, MEA

Akinola Akintunde, iProspect, Account Manager

Stephanie Ume, iProspect, Account Exec.

Glenfiddich Where Next?

Background

Glenfiddich is the world's most awarded single malt whiskey and for 130 years the brand has constantly challenged the status quo & pushed the boundaries. Glenfiddich recently launched into the Nigerian market but has grown to become the #1 selling single malt whisky with a strong on trade presence. Despite this growth, brand awareness is still relatively low compared to its key competitors. Glenfiddich also needed to build emotional connection with consumers and elevate its luxury credentials through effective deployment of the brand's creative assets. We were briefed to deliver an integrated media strategy and plan for Glenfiddich Nigeria and demonstrate how this will be applied across the various media channels. We were also required to provide a rationale for the media/channel choices. Due to the low awareness and early brand life stage in the market, the Stag's Story was essential to drive distinctive brand assets value, and increase likelihood of higher mental availability.

Creative Idea

The Glenfiddich Where Next campaign was created with an aim to inspire consumers to step out of their comfort zone, encouraging them to embrace risk in order to grow by continually asking themselves, Where Next?

The campaign idea celebrates the growth that can come through continually taking risks. To build meaning for the brand we identified a key distinctive brand asset, which was the logo/stag - as a key distinctive element that possesses a unique ability to become prominent enough to increase associative memory networks and further establish mental availability for Glenfiddich. Bringing this to life required that we enable a rich storytelling experience in our communications through innovative executions that truly embodies our Maverick Spirit. In summary we sought to build on brand equity, with the goal of creating stature and meaning at scale and while establishing Glenfiddich as a motivating symbol of taking risks to grow.

Strategy

Our strategy was to create a brand message so distinctive and relevant that it attracts far beyond its current base.

Our target audience are Mavericks of both genders. They consider themselves a work in progress – always striving for self-growth, learning new skills, and challenging their own views. Our Mavericks were categorized into three (3) broad groups. The 90% target – Maverick Crowds are light buyers of the category but represent a broad consumption pool. The 9% target – Irrepressible Mavericks are change makers who already have a strong affinity to our luxury values and position. The 1% target – Maverick Influencers are a small group of people with a big reach and impact on the wider population. The approach was to engage deeply with our 1% & 9% to generate advocacy while spreading our message far as possible across the 90% via paid & earned media while actively seeking conversion.

Execution

As a luxury brand, we could not compromise media quality for reach/cost, hence we aimed for premium positioning, beautiful formats, and a flawless end to end experience across all touch points. Using Dentsu's proprietary tool CCS, we could see this audience is one that likes to continually learn new things, showing strong penetration across the lines of technology and innovation and strong indexes for News, Politics and Documentaries. Our tools and insights led us to identifying broad reach channels that allow more emotional storytelling such as online video, advocacy, TV, social and OOH. To penetrate the 90% Maverick Crowd, we deployed short form online video, audiovisual on TV and high impact Out of Home. For the 9% Irrepressible Mavericks we utilized standout Out of Home executions, online video, lifestyle magazines, content partnerships with influencers tagged the #GLENFIDDICHWHERENEXTLIVE series which featured real stories and inspirational memoirs from true Maverick spirits.

Results

Overall, the Glenfiddich Where Next campaign reached over 40M+ across TV, OOH and Digital. The TV commercial was placed on high attention TV programming across status building channels with high scale such as National Geographic, CNN, ESPN etc. and we achieved 921 GRPs across Open and Pay TV. Aside from client feedback pertaining to the standout execution and cost savings achieved through extensive negotiations, the special builds OOH executions were recognized and applauded by consumers on social media as an impactful way to stand out from the regular OOH formats. Social and mobile ads placed in socially native ways and speaking to different social media consumption behaviours resulted in top results such as the cost per instream view of $0.0087, which is a very positive result compared to the industry benchmark of $0.02. A study conducted by Facebook post-campaign shows a strong brand lift was recorded during the period of the campaign when compared to brands in same vertical. Standard ad recall and ad favorability amongst the test group was +22.1% and +31.1% respectively.

BRAND	IOM - International Organisation for Migration
ENTRANT COMPANY	Now Available Africa, Accra, Ghana
AWARD	Bronze

No Place Like Home

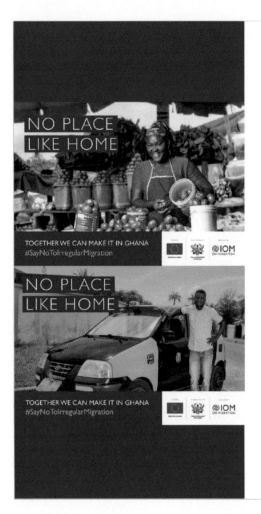

IOM

PROJECT BACKGROUND

The International Organisation for Migration has been in the business of promoting and raising awareness about regular migration for years. As a related organisation to the UN, IOM works in countries across the world to help ensure the orderly and humane management of migration.

In a 2018 survey, it came to light that, many young people from mostly rural and sub-urban regions in Ghana were risking their lives through irregular migration. To stop this trend, IOM in partnership with Ghana Immigration Service, Ministry of Interior and the Ghana Labour Commission joined forces with Now Available Africa to create a campaign that raises awareness about the dangers of irregular migration and the benefits of their resettlement efforts to many returnees in the country.

OUR TASK

We created a very emotional campaign broke through the myth that says: 'the grass is greener on the other side' and deepened the attachment to home as a place where real status, success and acceptance is found.

ROLLOUT AND MEDIA

We used a multi-channel mix to bring our big idea: NO PLACE LIKE HOME to life.
We kickstarted our campaign with an online press-launch; a first-of-its-kind in IOM Ghana and followed up with 2 real-life documentaries 2 short videos OOH Press Radio commercials and interactive programming, Mobile, A host of other online engagements and on-ground community events, we connected with our audience in meaningful ways.

The campaign launched at the beginning of 2020 and with the Covid-19 pandemic in full swing, our campaign pushed the issue of irregular migration to the forefront of national conversation and forced our audience to look within and see a positive image of a Ghana, full of possibilities.

50M+ ONLINE AND OFFLINE IMPRESSIONS

100k+ TOTAL INTERACTIONS

15% ONLINE ENGAGEMENT RATE

14% AD RECALL RATE (OFFLINE ACTIVITIES)

Credits

Emmanuel Amankwah, Now Available Africa, Creative Director

Betsey Osuteye, Now Available Africa, Senior Account Manager

Yvonne Acheampong, Now Available Africa, Client Service Director

Venus Tawiah, Now Available Africa, Director, Business and Communications

Emeka Dele, Now Available Africa, Media Strategist

Isaac Fuseini, Now Available Africa, Production Manager

Whitney Dena Thompson, Now Available Africa, Senior Social Media Manager

No Place Like Home

Background
The International Organisation for Migration has been in the business of promoting and raising awareness about regular migration for years. As a related organisation to the UN, IOM works in countries across the world to help ensure the orderly and humane management of migration. In a 2018 survey, it came to light that, many young people from mostly rural and sub-urban regions in Ghana were risking their lives through ir-regular migration. To stop this trend, IOM in partnership with Ghana Immigration Service, Ministry of Interior and the Ghana Labour Com-mission joined forces with Now Available Africa to create a campaign that raises awareness about the dangers of irregular migration and the benefits of their resettlement efforts to many returnees in the country.

Creative Idea
Using our Creative Idea: NO PLACE LIKE HOME, We created a very emotional campaign that broke through the myth that says: 'the grass is greener on the other side' and deepened the attachment to home as a place where real status, success and acceptance is found.

Strategy
The campaign launched at the beginning of 2020 and with the Covid-19 pandemic in full swing, our campaign pushed the issue of irregular migration to the forefront of national conversation and forced our audience to look within and see a positive image of a Ghana, full of possibilities.

Execution
We used a multi-channel mix to bring our big idea: NO PLACE LIKE HOME to life. We kickstarted our campaign with an online press-launch; a first-of-its-kind in IOM Ghana and followed up with 2 real-life docu-mentaries, 2 online videos, social meida, OOH , press, radio commercials, radio interviews, interactive programming, mobile, a host of other online engagements and on-ground community events, we connected with our audience in meaning-ful ways.

Results
50M+ Online and Offline Impressions
100K + Total Interactions
15% Online Engagement Rate
14% Ad Recall Rate (Offline)

Credits

Christina Ogoussan, Now Available Africa, Social Media Manager

Nanaesi Allotey, Now Available Africa, Traffic Manager

Frank Out, Now Available Africa, Art Director

Collins Owusu-Duku, Now Available Africa, Design and Video graphics

Selase Fiakpui, Now Available Africa, Copywriter

Venus Tawiah, Now Available Africa, Motion Graphics and Design

BRAND   HERO LAGER CLAN CAN
ENTRANT COMPANY VIZEUM Nigeria, GRA, Ikeja, Nigeria
AWARD   Shortlist

HERO LAGER CLAN CAN

Credits

Joshua Igbasan, VIZEUM Nigeria, Account Manager

Ayobami Adewale, VIZEUM Nigeria, Account Executive

Korede Ladejobi, VIZEUM Nigeria, Outdoor Manager

Akinola Akintunde, VIZEUM Nigeria, Digital Media Performance Manager

Stephanie Ume, VIZEUM Nigeria, Digital Media Performance Executive

Samuel Adeniyi, VIZEUM Nigeria, Account Executive

Emeka Okeke, VIZEUM Nigeria, Group Managing Director

Yetunde Adegbite, VIZEUM Nigeria, Managing Director

Theresa Ogah, VIZEUM Nigeria, Associate Media Director

HERO LAGER CLAN CAN

Background
Situation:
Culture plays a vital role for the people of South-Eastern Nigeria (The Igbos); they have a deep connection to their culture. However, there was a realization that westernization and other societal demands were beginning to make them lose sight of their background, their identity & especially their culture…the things that make them 'tick'!

This is a wake up call for the custodians of the culture, of the need to uphold their heritage and also remind them of their duties & responsibilities as sons & daughters of the soil.

Brief:
Drive meaning for the brand through strategic amplification of the Clan Can limited edition, while engaging & educating the audience about the 5 cultural appellations

Objectives:
- Through consistent & tailor-made messaging, nudge the people back to their heritage, reminding them of their identity, duties & responsibilities
- Entrench HERO Lager in the minds of the consumers as the Brand that identifies with their lifestyle & passion

Creative Idea
The idea is to create an intersection in the audience passion points: beer & culture. We therefore launched the "HERO CLAN CAN" - A Limited Edition packaging, first of its kind, with branded Igbo cultural insignia of Igwe, Odogwu, Dike, Nwanne & Ada (which are the 5 major appellations that represent the different great personalities of the Igbo culture & history) on the cans & bottles of Hero Lager.

These 5 Insignia are the pillars of their culture; representative of the different roles they all play in upholding their cultural values, thus:

ADA: The strong woman with a big heart
ODOGWU: The one who represents his people wherever he is
NWANNE: That guy who is always quick to lend a helping hand
DIKE: The defender! That man who always has your back
IGWE: The leader!

Having these inscribed on the product package creates a deep emotional connection, is very relatable to the consumer & extensively brings about an awakening in the people about their culture even as they consume the brand

Strategy
Accounting for over 57% of the entire national spend on alcohol consumption, according to a 2019 report by the Nigeria Bureau of Statistics, the consumers in these markets (S/East & S/South) are undoubtedly heavy & passionate drinkers who do not joke with their consumption moments, as they serve as a pivot for personal identification & social interaction.

The core consumers are both Male & Female, age 18-39 & predominantly middle to lower class (CD SEC). Their motivation is money, success and being recognition of same.
Their consumption of media is predominantly Radio, OOH & TV, with affinity for entertainment & sports contents, with indigenous rendition.
They are emotionally connected to their roots & culture, while their functional need is a rich satisfying beer that enhances enjoyable moments with friends

The strategy was to drive meaning, create awareness & connect to the audience passion points via tactical use of high-impact & engaging platforms & emotionally-driven contents

Execution
EVENTS:
The Can Clan was launched with an event – a cultural concert – tagged Hero Fiesta, to unveil the Clan Can in grand style with performances from renowned celebrities from the region.

RADIO:
To engage the audience, educate & drive meaning, we leveraged Radio (the most consumed medium by the TG based on audience media consumption analysis) via indigenous content curation/sponsorship

OOH:
Lamp-poles Di-Cuts with the different designs/appellations of the Clan Cans was executed along high footfall routes & points of consumption

DIGITAL:
The digital assets chaselist included cutdowns of 6, 15 & 30sec videos and pre-roll creatives. We deployed Online Videos, Social Media execution, Influencer engagements and Third-party platforms.

TELEVISION:
The crux of TV execution was partnerships with indigenous Igbo contents to efficiently drive campaign meaning & impact & ROS placements

Results
HERO Lager gained the highest SOV in its core Regions:
(S/East: 88%; S/South: 74%)

Despite being a regional brand, the brand still gained the highest overall Category Share of Voice (66%) in the beer category even over all national brands, during the period of the campaign.

On digital, we achieved 2x of our planned KPIs, hitting about 29.1 million+ impressions with 1.3M+ audience engagements. Campaign also delivered over 2.4M views & 1.6m+ Reach. We also leveraged location targeted SMS to penetrate regions with low internet usage.

The brand achieved a Market Share growth of 2.1%; Year-on-Year Sales Growth of 18%; 1.8% Brand Power growth & 4% increase in Brand Trial

Credits

Marian Ogaziechi, VIZEUM Nigeria, Associate Media Director

Tolulope Adedeji, International Breweries Plc, Marketing Director

Margaret Igabali, International Breweries Plc, Marketing Manager

Chibuikem Uzochukwu, International Breweries Plc, Brand Manager

Chuka Nnaobi, International Breweries Plc, Connections Manager

PR & Reputation **Management**

BRAND   Mayor of Djougou
ENTRANT COMPANY   Opinion&Public, Abidjan, Ivory Coast
AWARD   Bronze

Local Solutions Against Global Pandemic

Credits

Kwame Senou, Opinion & Public, PR Counsel

Local Solutions Against Global Pandemic

Background

Like the whole world, Djougou the 3rd most populated city in Benin Republic, was dealing with the COVID-19 pandemic that was depleting its ressources and creating major challenges for the residents of the community and the administration. Unfortunately Benin followed the same approach many governments took which was to have a national response coordinated directly from the capital city with no local direction

The Mayor of Djougou presented the problem to his PR agency that suggested an initiative to influence the government in updating its approach and allocate ressources to the city of Djougou.

Creative Idea

Local Initiatives against Global Pandemic

The idea was to showcase how effectives are local initiatives against a global pandemic that has a lot to do with behavior change. Playing with local and global, was building on the glocal strategy known to the private which the President of Benin Republic and many of his advisers are from.

Strategy

The strategy was to publish an Op-Ed in a major panafrican newspaper to drive a media storm in order to pressure the government of Benin Republic to allocate grants to local communities to fight the pandemic with their local initiatives.

The media selection was done based on the preferred media used by the central government and its various agencies to

communicate or publish their press release.

Execution

The Op-Ed was published on Monday, July 13th 2020 by Financial Afrik magazine's website, a leading francophone Africa media that was known to be frequently read by the Finance Minister of Benin who won an award twice from the news outlet.

The Op-Ed was then suggested to many beninese media for republishing in order to drive a media storm and was shared across social media on Facebook, WhatsApp and the political WhatsApp groups that are very effective in driving information to the highest levels of the government.

Result

More than 10 media offline and online published the Op-Ed, Key Opinion Leaders shared on their social media. From the Mayor's social media assets, it reached over 20,000 people with organic reach.

Pressured both by the media storm and the need to take immediate action, the central government of the Republic of Benin granted the city of Djougou a special allowance of about USD $150,000 to fight the spread of Covid-19.

The success of the action was such that the government instructed other cities and regions in Benin to implement the same strategy, with special grants in excess of 7 millions US$ from the central government.

BRAND   Guinness Ghana (A Diageo Company)

ENTRANT COMPANY   mediaReach OMD, Accra, Ghana

AWARD   Bronze

Yen Nhyin Baom

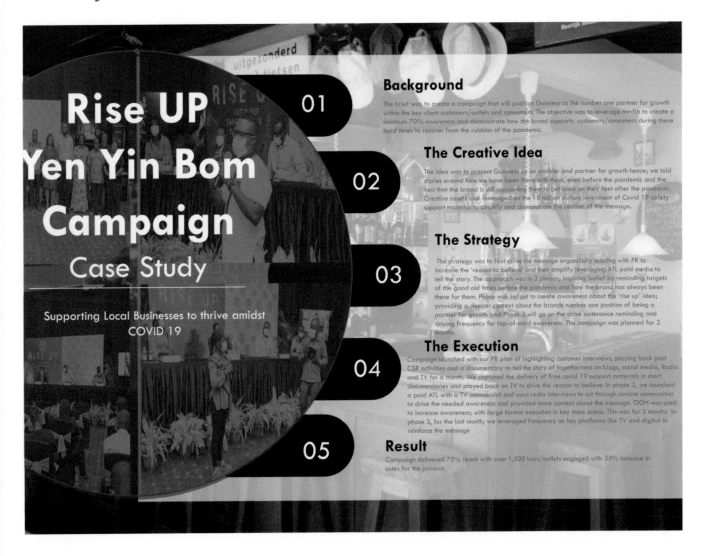

Rise UP Yen Yin Bom Campaign
Case Study

Supporting Local Businesses to thrive amidst COVID 19

01

Background

The brief was to create a campaign that will position Guinness as the number one partner for growth within the key client customers/outlets and consumers. The objective was to leverage media to create a minimum 70% awareness and demonstrate how the brand supports customers/consumers during these hard times to recover from the rubbles of the pandemic.

02

The Creative Idea

The idea was to present Guinness as an enabler and partner for growth hence; we told stories around how we have been there with them, even before the pandemic and the fact that the brand is still supporting them to get back on their feet after the pandemic. Creative assets also leveraged on the 10 million dollars investment of Covid 19 safety support material to amplify and demonstrate the realism of the message.

03

The Strategy

The strategy was to first drive the message organically leading with PR to increase the 'reason to believe' and then amplify leveraging ATL paid media to tell the story. The approach was in 3 phases; inspiring belief by reminding targets of the good old times before the pandemic and how the brand has always been there for them. Phase was set out to create awareness about the 'rise up' idea; providing a deeper context about the brands number one position of being a partner for growth and Phase 3 will go on the drive sustenance reminding and driving frequency for top-of-mind awareness. The campaign was planned for 3 months.

04

The Execution

Campaign launched with our PR plan of highlighting customer interviews, playing back past CSR activities and a documentary to tell the story of togetherness on blogs, social media, Radio and TV for a month. We captured the delivery of free covid 19 support materials in short documentaries and played back on TV to drive the reason to believe. In phase 2, we launched a paid ATL with a TV commercial and used radio interviews to cut through remote communities to drive the needed awareness and provided more context about the message. OOH was used to increase awareness; with large format execution in key mass areas. This was for 2 months In phase 3, for the last month; we leveraged frequency on key platforms like TV and digital to reinforce the message

05

Result

Campaign delivered 75% reach with over 1,500 bars/outlets engaged with 35% increase in sales for the product.

Credits

Gideon Quaku, OMD, Team Lead

Justina Kortly, OMD, Planner

David Agbeviade, OMD, Buyer

Taniya Mondal, OMD, Account Director

David Ofosuhene, OMD, Head of Strategy

Magdaline Afutu, PHD, Planner

Yen Nhyin Baom

Background

Following the devastating effect of COVID 19 for the world at large, Ghanaians were not left out of the impact of this pandemic. Many businesses responded in different ways to tackle the problem including remedial measures to save cost and stay afloat by all means. Our category was one of the most affected especially during the lockdown which crippled sales and revenue but we realized that this was not just about us as a business, it also affected all of our customers (the business connected to our sales and distribution network) and their families. As everyone tried to bounce back post-COVID, we realized the need to walk the talk and truly support our loyal customers who are, in reality, our partners in progress

Creative Idea

We sought to approach things differently and launched our special empowerment campaign "Yen Yin Bom" which means Partner for Growth. This campaign aimed to support local distributor businesses to thrive post COVID and position Guinness as the number one partner for growth among our key customers not just in words but in action. The idea was to present Guinness as an enabler and partner for growth hence; we told stories around how we have been there with them, even before the pandemic and the fact that the brand is still supporting them to get back on their feet after the pandemic. Creative assets also leveraged on the 10 million dollars investment of Covid 19 safety support material to amplify and demonstrate the realism of the message.

Strategy

The strategy was to spotlight specific partners. The strategy was to first drive the message organically leading with PR to increase the 'reason to believe' and then amplify leveraging ATL paid media to tell the story. The approach was in 3 phases; inspiring belief by reminding targets of the good old times before the pandemic and how the brand has always been there for them. Phase was set out to create awareness about the 'rise up' idea; providing a deeper context about the brands number one position of being a partner for growth and Phase 3 will go on the drive sustenance reminding and driving frequency for top-of-mind awareness. The campaign was planned for 3 months.

Execution

Campaign launched with our PR plan of highlighting customer interviews, playing back past CSR activities and a documentary to tell the story of togetherness on blogs, social media, Radio and TV for a month. We captured the delivery of free covid 19 support materials in short documentaries and played back on TV to drive the reason to believe. In phase 2, we launched a paid ATL with a TV commercial and used radio interviews to cut through remote communities to drive the needed awareness and provided more context about the message. OOH was used to increase awareness; with large format execution in key mass areas. This was for 2 months In phase 3, for the last month; we leveraged frequency on key platforms like TV and digital to reinforce the message.

Results

Campaign delivered 75% reach with over 1,500 partners engaged. This resulted in increases sales 35% over projection for the period.

BRAND	TBWA \Concept
ENTRANT COMPANY	TBWA \Concept, Ikeja, Lagos
AWARD	Shortlist

End SARS Campaign

Open
Happiness.
But mothers sadly close
caskets because of SARS.

We bought your slogans.
Now buy into ours.
Speak up to **#ENDSARS**

Credits

Wayne Samuel, TBWA\Concept, Copywriter

Kel Nwuke, TBWA\Concept, Art Director

Chinwe Onuoha, TBWA\Concept, Copy Manger

Yusuf Adejumo, TBWA\Concept, Dep. Creative Director

End SARS Campaign

Background

TBWA/Concept is a full time advertising agency in Nigeria known for her great creativity and disruptive ideas. But over time, the company lost its spark and became a shadow of itself.

The Challenge

Let the world know that we still got it.

Creative Idea

They say in every challenge, there's an opportunity to shine. The End SARS campaign of 2020 presented a great opportunity for the creative agency to showcase its creativity. Now, while the youths were speaking out against police brutality in a loud voice, corporate Nigeria was very silent. and this silence was felt across the nation. Every one hated their silence, but none had the balls to call them out.

Strategy

How do we call out brands without calling them out? We speak their language.

Target Audience- Corporate Nigeria across different levels

Target Media- Social Media

Execution

Brands have a voice- it's in their color, tone of voice, taglines etc. the idea is to speak to them in the language they will understand- their own.

Results

Over 10,000 organic impressions across the different social media platforms. the campaign was shared and retweeted severally without spending a dime, some brands eventually joined the conversation and spoke up against the brutality, but most importantly, people appreciated and celebrated the creativity, the agency got 5 new accounts 3 months after the campaign.

Credits

Biose Isichie, TBWA\Concept, Digital Strategist

Dotun Falade, TBWA\Concept, Digital Strategist

Oyinda Fakile, TBWA\Concept, Creative Director

Ranti Atunwa, TBWA\Concept, Exec. Creative Director

BRAND   Sanlam

ENTRANT COMPANY   King James Group, Cape Town, South Africa

AWARD   Gold

The Olympian

Credits

Alistair King, King James, Chief Creative Officer

Matt Ross, King James, Executive Creative Director

Devin Kennedy, King James, Executive Creative Director

Jared Osmond, King James, Creative Director

Cameron Watson, King James, Creative Director

Kathi Jones, King James, Agency producer

Paul Ward, Giant Films, Director

Martina Shieder, Giant Films, Producer

Sean Henekom, King James, Business Unit Director

Jovana Harkhu, King James, Group Account Director

Taryn Walker, King James, Managing Director

Rosemary Boronetti, King James, Strategist

Anthony Lee Martin, Me&My Friends, Editor

Lauren Chavez, King James, Earned Media Specialist

Jade Lotriet, King James, Earned Media Specialist

Simon Kohler, Field Audio, Sound Engineer

Nicolaas van Reenen, Field Audio, Sound Engineer

Deon van Zyl, Freelance, Director of photography

Nic Apostoli, Strangelove Studios, Colourist

Charmaine Greyling, Strangelove Studios, Flame Artist

Darian Simon, Strangelove Studios, Flame Artist

Caitlin Rooskrantz, JGC Gymnastics, Performer

Paul Spiers, New Creation Collective, Editor

Colleen Knox, New Creation Collective, Editor

Riaan Myburg, New Creation Collective, VFX Artist

Anthony Murray, King James, Retouching Artist

Amy Knight, New Creation Collective, Post Producer

Leticha Kisting, King James, Producer

Daniel Zoeller, King James, Animator

Emma Drummond, King James, Digital Group Head

Joe Van Schalkwyk, King James, Digital Designer

Liezl Fourie, King James, Digital Designer

Miles Davis, King James, Digital Designer

Sue Waters, King James, Campaign Producer

Annemarie Blaensdorf, King James, Project Manager

Rudi Pottas, King James, Project Manager

Emma Rassmussen, King James, Project Manager

The Olympian

Background

Sonatel Orange Group is the historical operator and leader in Senegal, also present in Mali, Guinea, Guinea Bissau and Sierra Leone. Although the group is very involved in the fields of education, the environment, culture and health through its foundation and its numerous CSR actions, its institutional image reflects its economic success rather than its societal commitment.

Creative Idea
Insight

Every year a girl stays at school, her future earnings increase between 10% to 20%.
In Senegal, girls outnumber boys and have better results at middle school.
But at the University girls make only 40% of total student population due to various social barriers.
Challenge
Commit to keeping girls in school and make Sonatel Orange the Herald of this issue.
Creative idea
Engaging the community through emotion (Film fiction "On the way to school – Format 2mn et 4mn) and sharing experience (Social Experience) broadcasted only on digital)
A platform (HumanInsideAfrica.com) that highlights the commitments of Sonatel Group and especially that for keeping girls in school through testimonies and true stories.
#JigeenJangal (Girl Learn)

Strategy

Our strategy with this campaign for the «Keeping girls in school» was to encourage it into a more engage Human centric discourse, to tell stories to start the conversation and mobilize in order to (re)position itself as a major player in Social Development.
Media strategy (off and online) : low expenses and a lot of effects.
The campaign's offline media budget (tele-Radio-Press) is less than €40,000. In digital, the media budget is €0. 2 live talks with 5 influencers, who signed up for free, made the film viral and started the conversation. The first livetalk took place the day before the launch, with the film being shown in preview on a TV set where a representative of the brand to discuss with education specialists. The 2nd Livetalk took place on the day of the launch and triggered many conversations where the #JingeeJangal was widely used: 33 million impressions in less than 10 hours.
Execution
The launch of the campaign took place on the eve of World Education Day with a TV platform sponsored by the brand dedicated to girls' education in Senegal.
On this set the leaders of the group intervened.
The emotional film "On the Way to School" was premiered, launching the conversation around #JigeenJangale. On D-Day (February 24, «World Education Day») the film was broadcast on TV and social media with a call to action inviting people to visit the humaninsideafrica.com platform, listen to the podcasts and share their experiences as well. In radio, we also activated by broadcasting excerpts of podcasts testimonies inviting listeners to connect. On D+3 a series of stories were broadcast on Facebook and Instagram referring to the web platform. The conversation essentially focused on Twitter with an effective influence strategy. On D+8 we then activated the second part. That of the experience with the broadcast of the film «testimonials» on our online channels.

Result

A positive, activist and action-oriented digital conversation hailed by all for its relevance and the emotion it generated, the #JiggeenJangal campaign generated an impressive stream of spontaneous testimonies. Young girls, women, but also fathers, brothers, or fellow students told of the barriers, the stops, the injustices, the broken dreams or, on the contrary, the paths of hope and pride that they experienced or crossed. These numerous testimonies opened the way to a change of mentality but also to proposals, Relationships or supportive and inspiring initiatives such as bringing highly educated women into schools to talk to young girls about trades and guidance, etc. The Jigeen Jangale campaign showed the Sonatel Orange group from a new perspective, sharing a unifying, modern and positive vision of society. Its willingness to accompany change with a strong voice was all the more perceived as it was legitimate in view of its long-standing support for girls' schooling, the digital inclusion of women and a gender-sensitive human resources policy. #JingeenJangal has federated speech and demonstrated that a societal and committed momentum can make things happen. As of March 30, 2020, the campaign reached more than 60% of the population in TV and radio and reached over :
- 6,200 mentions of the hashtag ;
- 30,900 interactions ;
- 132 Millions in digital of impressions.

Use of **Data**

BRAND   Safaricom PLC
ENTRANT COMPANY   Dentsu Aegis Network, Nairobi, Kenya
AWARD   Gold

The Bantering Billboard

Credits

Gideon Ruita, Dentsu Aegis Network – Kenya, Account Director

Alex Tutu, Dentsu Aegis Network – Kenya, Managing Director

Miriam Waititu, Dentsu Aegis Network – Kenya, Business Unit Head

Stuti Ahuja, Safaricom PLC, Brand

Amelia Aganda, Safaricom PLC, Marketing

Stella Arithi, Safaricom PLC, Marketing

Carolyne Kendi, Safaricom PLC, Marketing

The Bantering Billboard

Background
Safaricom, the biggest telecommunications company in Kenya, was celebrating their 20-year anniversary and they wanted to make it about making it about their consumers and engaging with their consumers. Their message to Kenyans was two simple words: "Twende Tukiuke", meaning, "Let's go beyond."
So, we set out to bring the message home to each one of them, with a first of its kind out of home execution.

Creative Idea
Safaricom was looking for a way to make its 20th anniversary celebrations all about their customers. We therefore looked for an opportunity that would not only celebrate it's anniversary but also engage with our audiences like never before. Enter the Bantering billboard. A billboard that would not only customise messages to our audiences but one that would also elicit responses from them.

Strategy
Using data from Google Mobility, we were able to identify Nairobi's busiest round about that would offer us the ample dwell time to run our execution. We then used KURA (Kenya Urban Roads Authority) data to identify the peak traffic hours where we could engage with motorists stuck in traffic. Using data from the camera and through machine learning we were able to convert a normal display DOOH screen in to an interactive platform with our audiences.

Execution
We installed a camera on the digital screen at the University Way round about facing inbound traffic. The Camera, using AI, machine learning installed on the screen was able to identify the make colour and model of the vehicles and customise a shout out to the motorists based on the above metrics. The message on the screen also broke down what "Kiuke" meant to Kenyan commuters and in the end asked them to hoot twice or give a response to signal that they understood.

Results
We had over 28000 customised messages to motorists and reached a peak of 58000 impressions daily from interaction with the screen.

Use of Influencers & **Brand Ambassadors**

BRAND   International Breweries
ENTRANT COMPANY   Mediafuse Dentsu - Vizeum, Ikeja
AWARD   Shortlist

Budweiser Kings of Football Show

Credits

Joshua Oyeleye, Vizeum, Media Manager

Olajumoke Okikiolu, IB PLC, Marketing Manager

Olajumoke Ajayi, Vizeum, Media Executive

Akinola Akintunde, iProspect, Digital Account Manager

Samuel Adeniyi, Vizeum, Media Buying

Lanre Ojoawo, Super Sport, Director

Ini Marshal, Super Sport, Producer

Tayo Bayo, Super Sport, Co-Producer

Nana Fischer, Isobar, Account Manager

Chinonso Wilson, Isobar, Account Executive

Halima Bakenne, Isobar, Content Manager

Kehinde Allen Isobar Art Director

Chuka Nnaobi, IB PLC, Connections Manager

Tolulope Adedeji, IB PLC, Marketing Director

Dubem Orji, IB PLC, Brand Manager

Tochukwu Macfoy, StoryLab, Entertainment Specialist

Siboniso Ngubane, Super Sport, Production Director

Pooven Chetty, Super Sport, Sales Director

Budweiser Kings of Football Show

Background

The Budweiser Kings of Football show was created to elevate the position of the brand as official sponsors of the English Premier League and La Liga and grow SOV on Supersport (#1 Football Entertainment platform in Africa).

We were set to launch the second phase of the 2020/21 football season campaign in January 2021, however learnings from the past executions showed that we had some challenge with cut through and engagement. It was clear we had to improve the entertainment factor and appeal of the show. To optimize the show, we decided to test four (4) different TV show concepts. Following the test, we discovered that consumers were showing a higher preference for shows where they can have a voice. Fan involvement stood as a very important factor, consumers wanted an environment of socializing and friendly rivalry. By engaging the right influencer and gamifying the situation, we created a social strategy that helped to re-energize football fans all over Nigeria.

Creative Idea

Introducing the new Kings of Football Game Show, the ultimate lifestyle and football trivia game show!

The new Kings of football show was created to bring football fans closer to the greatness on and off the pitch to inspire them to seize their opportunity and celebrate their time to shine. Three (3) hosts and six (6) consumers will grace the stage every week till the end of the 2020/21 football season. The six (6) contestants will form two (2) teams who will compete against each other for a 1Million naira prize to be given away on every episode. The contestants will be tested on their knowledge about everything Football from the English premier league to the Spanish La Liga. The game show was structured into two halves like a typical soccer match, with categories such as Kick Off, Through Pass, VAR, Penalty etc. During the half time we create engagement using Fantasy Premier League, Fans Zone Vox Pop and Skype Call sessions with celebs and pundits.

Strategy

Our strategy was to create a TV show so distinctive and relevant that it attracts far beyond its current base. And we intended to achieve this by establishing ourselves as a brand that brings fans closer to the greatness on and off the pitch inspiring them to seize opportunity and celebrate their time to shine. For the first phase of the relaunch show we focused on embedding a cultural layer, aiming to win the hearts of more football fans between the ages of 18-44. Major brand ambassadors were selected to tease the announcement of the new Brand Ambassador, leveraging their potential appeal to a broader audience. For the second phase, the brand announced Ozo as a new Brand Ambassador with comms on Radio and Social Media. The third phase had Ozo make his first appearance as co-host on the KOF Game show which premiered on the 28th of February 2021.

Execution

Hardly any other medium reaches the football loving beer drinkers as accurately as Super Sport, Africa's first 24/7 Sports broadcaster. So together with Super Sport, we developed and co-produced the Kings of Football Show, a one-hour TV game show recorded every Thursday and premiered on Sundays. The show is hosted by two male hosts (Jimmie and Ozo) and a female host (Ose) who are always in the company of the resident DJ Dips always keeping the energy levels up and up. Over eight (8) Sundays, Budweiser has presented the most engaging football gameshow ever seen on TV. From opening graphics, verbal mentions, quality of questions, set design and custom vox pop content, Budweiser dominated this premium, one-hour time block as well as various other repeat slots on across Super Sport channels every week. Consumers who want to participate are encouraged to register on www.budweiserngeria.com.ng/kofshow and each participating team stands a chance to win up to 1M naira on every episode.

Results

Budweiser Kings of Football Show was the #1 TV show on Super Sport primetime besides live football matches, with an average rating of 4.7 (MF, ABC, 18-44) recording a viewership growth of (+16% YOY) within the first month of evaluation. Social media was also full of praise as Ozo's reveal as the brand's new BA and co-host of the KOF show generated over 14,000 tweets with over 96% positive sentiment and 82.5% predominant emotion on joy. On the 28th of February 2021, when the new edition of the Budweiser Kings of Football show went live with the brand's newest ambassador, Ozo, as new co-host. The results were phenomenal in numbers and conversation on social media, especially Twitter. Budweiser created such huge positive PR buzz across social media with both hashtags #BudFootball & #KingsofFootballShow becoming #1 twitter trending topic in Nigeria.

The KOF Show crew have visited 4 (four) bars in eight (8) weeks and interviewed over 30 fans on the KOF Fans Zone Vox Pop segment. The entire Football campaign has aided Budweiser to reach 18.2MM+ people within the campaign period.

BRAND   NBC Universal
ENTRANT COMPANY   Ogilvy, Lagos, Nigeria
AWARD   Shortlist

Telemundo Africa Tik Tok Launch

Credits

Chidera Okehi, Ogilvy Nigeria, Social Media Manager

Topher Willis, NBC Universal, Client

Tik Tok Tik Tok, Social Media Manager, Collaborating company

Telemundo Africa Tik Tok Launch

Background

Telemundo Africa wanted to launch it's Tik-Tok channel in Africa and so the create awareness for the page, Telemundo Africa used the premiere of a brand new season of a super anticipated show, Iron Rose 2.

The main character on the show Iron Rose, Altagracia Sandoval was a Boss lady who was super fashionable. She is not afraid to wear her heels, Red lipstick and the outfits that make her stand out to a shootout.
We told fans to rub their red lipstick like the Boss lady will while dancing to song chosen for the campaign - Say Cheese.

Our Target audience was Passionistas aged 25 - 35 who have Tik-Tok accounts and want more from the Brand. The Target media used was Tik-Tok. The plan included use of Heavy Tik-Tok female influencers from all over Africa. We used Talents (actors from Iron Rose) Kika Edgar, Aracely Arambula and a few passionistas to create the first set of videos to show fans in a promo video what we expect from them.

Execution

The campaign was executed with Influencers around Africa, most of which were Nigerians to suit our priority TA - Lily Afe, Laura Ikeji, Juliet Ibrahim, Iyabo Ojo etc. Kidi Music's song titled Say Cheese was used include our Ghanian audience. We ran the campaign from June - August and different assets were used to push promotions at different stages. Promo Videos, Placement ads on header and page takeover on the Tik-Tok app. Instagram and Facebook assets to cross promote the campaign and create awareness.

Results

The campaign hashtag #IronRoseChallenge was used over 2.5m times and Telemundo gained over 4,000 new fans on Tik-Tok.

Credits

Chidera Okehi, Ogilvy Nigeria, Social Media Manager

Topher Willis, NBC Universal, Client

Tik Tok Tik Tok, Social Media Manager, Collaborating company

BRAND   Guinness Ghana Breweries (Diageo)
ENTRANT COMPANY   Now Available Africa, Accra, Ghana
AWARD   Shortlist

Johnnie Walker's 200th

Credits

Emmanuel Amankwah, Now Available Africa, Creative Director

Yvonne Acheampong, Now Available Africa, Client Service Director

Venus Tawiah, Now Available Africa, Director, Business and Communications

Anna Agostinelli, Now Available Africa, Account Manager

Shaaibatu Abdul Rasheed, Now Available Africa, Social Media and Influencer Executive

Samira Saadu, Now Available Africa, Account Manager

Whitney Dena Thompson, Now Available Africa, Senior Social Media Manager

Christina Ogoussan, Now Available Africa, Social Media Manager

Emeka Dele, Now Available Africa, Media Strategist

Akwesi Wiredu Agyekum, Now Available Africa, Motion Graphics and Design

Johnnie Walker's 200th

Background

In light of Johnnie Walker's 200th celebration, our agency was tasked to help change the brand perception among new and emerging drinkers. For a long time, the brand has been perceived as Male-Pale-Stale. We decided to shift perceptions about the brand and position the brand as a more inclusive, not just male dominated, welcoming to the female drinker, young, classy and aspirational.

Creative Idea

Our big Idea for JW 200th was: Celebrating a Unique Journey. 200 years of Johnnie Walker is no mean achievement and as we celebrate a brand that has inspired many for years, we wanted to nring this celebration to our consumers in a memorable way. Johnnie Walker has always been about walking an steps that join together into making unique journeys. Our big idea celebrates this unique journey of our brand and the many individuals that it has inspired and continues to inch forward, towards thier goal. The influencers drew inspiration from this to create content.

Strategy

We selected an interesting mix of young, male and female lifestyle influencers. They were tasked with amplifying our content and creating additional, refreshing content that helped to celebrcte Johnnie Walker at 200. By doing this, we hoped to erase the old perception of the brand and make it more appealing to a young and trendy set of drinkers. Our strategy for the influencers were to use their platforms to build interest and conversations around the campaign and to share their experiences at House of Walker in order to drive footfall. 2 main categories of influencers were used- 7 main influencers who acted as the leading faces of the campaign and a group of micro influencers who focused mostly on House Of Walker activities.

Execution

These influencers helped move our audience purchase our special limited-edition bottles and pushed traffic to our one-of-a-kind Pop-Up Store - House of Walker. Together, they created content, they attended events and gave up-to-the-minute updates, they created cocktails using the products among other exciting activities that helped to make this iconic brand, the most desirable, most talked about and most engaging brand over the period of the celebration.

Results

64M+ Total Impressions, 76% Combined Reach, 88% of Total Target Reached.

The Johnnie Walker Instagram page grew from 300 to over a 1,000 followers within the period. Influencers were present at HOW Accra throughout the month, sharing content on live activities and ongoing in-store experiences. Consumers who didn't know about the brand were exposed to it through influencer content and activities. Micro influencers created exciting content that lead to the necessary buzz around the Pop-up. Engagement on our IG stories increased with our audiences tagging us in posts relating to the campaign/brand.

Credits

Audrey Quaye, Now Available Africa, Graphic Designer

Frank Otu Now Available Africa Art Director

Selase Fiakpui, Now Available Africa, Copywriter

Isaac Fuseini, Now Available Africa, Production Manager

Constance Afua Mensah, Now Available Africa, Traffic Manager

Lesego Lesbogang Mohale, Guinness Ghana Breweries PLC (Diageo), Portfolio Marketing Manager

Abena Chrappah, Guinness Ghana Breweries PLC (Diageo), Digital and Media Manager

Wilma Amoo-Osae, Guinness Ghana Breweries PLC (Diageo), Assistant Brand Manager

Abdul-Samed Sadiq, Guinness Ghana Breweries PLC (Diageo), Senior Brand Manager (Spirits)

BRAND   Sanlam
ENTRANT COMPANY King James Group, Cape Town, South Africa
AWARD   Gold

Gogo

Credits

Alistair King, King James, Chief Creative Officer

Matt Ross, King James, Executive Creative Director

Devin Kennedy, King James, Executive Creative Director

Jared Osmond, King James, Creative Director

Cameron Watson, King James, Creative Director

Kathi Jones, King James, Agency producer

Paul Ward, Giant Films, Director

Martina Shieder, Giant Films, Producer

Sean Henekom, King James, Business Unit Director

Jovana Harkhu, King James, Group Account Director

Taryn Walker, King James, Managing Director

Rosemary Boronetti, King James, Strategist

Anthony Lee Martin, Me&My Friends, Editor

Lauren Chavez, King James, Earned Media Specialist

Jade Lotriet, King James, Earned Media Specialist

Simon Kohler, Field Audio, Sound Engineer

Nicolaas van Reenen, Field Audio, Sound Engineer

Deon van Zyl, Freelance, Director of photography

Nic Apostoli, Strangelove Studios, Colourist

Charmaine Greyling, Strangelove Studios, Flame Artist

Gogo

Background

Elders are respected figures in many South African and African cultures. They're the voice of wisdom we turn to for guidance. When they talk, we listen (because they've got the life experience to back it up).

Creative Idea

We created Gogo – the wisest of grandmothers and someone authentic enough for the nation to trust for sound (often unsolicited) advice. She had the life experience to back up her opinions and instructions, and her message was always clear "time is precious". Her value of time tied in with the key benefit of Sanlam's funeral cover, namely that it pays out in just 4 hours. So Gogo urged consumers to make the most of their time, and plan for when another's time was over. And they listened.

Strategy

Funeral cover is one of the biggest grudge purchases for South Africans. It's something they don't want to think about or hear from others about. But in a country where many if not most are cash-strapped, the tragic and unexpected expected cost of providing a funeral for a loved one can be crippling without good cover. The challenge is to get people to listen when you talk to them about it.

Execution

Gogo became the first influencer to target the funeral product space, but no one was the wiser as to her mission until after she'd endeared herself to them. Social accounts, talk shows, cooking shows, personal gifs and memes: if influencers were doing it Gogo was doing it, and people loved it. All the while, she was establishing and reinforcing the value of time, building up to Sanlam's incorporation of the 4-hour funeral plan.

Results

341% increase in funeral plan leads
52189 total brand engagements
119+ million impressions

Credits

Darian Simon, Strangelove Studios, Flame Artist

Caitlin Rooskrantz, JGC Gymnastics, Performer

Paul Spiers, New Creation Collective, Editor

Colleen Knox, New Creation Collective, Editor

Riaan Myburg, New Creation Collective, VFX Artist

Anthony Murray, King James, Retouching Artist

Amy Knight, New Creation Collective, Post Producer

Leticha Kisting, King James, Producer

Daniel Zoeller, King James, Animator

Emma Drummond, King James, Digital Group Head

Joe Van Schalkwyk, King James, Digital Designer

Liezl Fourie, King James, Digital Designer

Miles Davis, King James, Digital Designer

Sue Waters, King James, Campaign Producer

Annemarie Blaensdorf, King James, Project Manager

Rudi Pottas, King James, Project Manager

Emma Rassmussen, King James, Project Manager

Use of Insights **& Strategy**

BRAND   GODREJ NIGERIA LIMITED
ENTRANT COMPANY   mediaReach OMD, Maryland, Lagos, Nigeria
AWARD   Silver

Darling Hair BBN

Credits

Titilayo Adebayo, mediaReach OMD, Media Buyer

Darling Hair BBN

Background

The country had been on a total lockdown for 3 months prior and this had caused a downturn in the sales of Darling Hair products in the markets as there was no motivation for people to make their hair at all, it was also impossible considering that beauty parlors were locked down based on the strong directives form the government to help curb the virus. As many people all over the world began to try out new things to keep busy, Nigerian women had no choice but to go the Do-It-Yourself route as regards beauty and personal grooming; this birthed the need for Darling Hair to encourage creative and individual use of her products.

Creative Idea

Many of the brand's target audience were already spending a lot of time on audio-visual platforms in a bid to learn and practice styling their hair by themselves. TV viewership had also increased massively during the pandemic and the popular reality TV show, Big Brother Naija was scheduled to return to screen in that time, we saw an opportunity to connect our products with the needs of consumers by bringing DIY footages to a bigger audience than Youtube.

Strategy

Targeting women between 18-45 years in the Social Economic Class B and C who are stylish and fashion progressive, it is important that we presented as a brand that understood her pain as the pandemic and lockdown were concerned. No aspect of life was business as usual and that included her beauty routines and personal grooming so we leveraged TV to communicate that we are with her through the times by adopting the DIY route at the Big Brother Naija Lockdown Edition. Instead of having professional hairstylists make the hair of the housemates, video footages were instead shown to the housemates detailing a step by step method of achieving popular hairdos.

Execution

Beyond running our TVC that amplified our theme and connected audience at high frequency, we had the Darling hair Exclusive salon open every Sunday morning to all housemates on the show to style their hair by themselves. Video clips were shown in the salon to demonstrate how to make different hairstyles. Because making one's hair by oneself is not an easy feat, we knew we had to encourage weekly participation from the housemates through incentives. They were scored on creativity and maintenance and the housemate with the overall score at the end of the season won the sum of 2M NGN. On one of the days in the house, we also tasked the housemates to showcase their creativity in a runway fashion show as well as a vogue-inspired photoshoot. They were asked to create "Africa themed hair styles" on one another and showcase these using props and costumes provided.

Results

1. The task had our hashtag "DarlinghairXBBN" trending on twitter all day with a lot of conversations generated by the viewers at home.
2. We launched the Darling Empress collection (human hair) and all our products were sold out within the first month of Launch.
3. 20% increase in our followers across all social media platforms.
4. Launched the online shopping and home delivery platform and this has resulted in the double size of sales of our products.

How did Insight Enhance the Campaign?

As a business, being there for your customers transcends meeting their immediate needs, it also means anticipating what they may need further down the line. Even though we were in the thick of the lockdown, Darling Hair showed their customers how to maintain their sense of style whilst adjusting to the new normal. By going the DIY route on the season's Big brother, we showed the audience how much more is possible and can be achieved despite the restriction on movement.

BRAND   Budweiser Nigeria
ENTRANT COMPANY   Isobar Nigeria, Lagos, Nigeria
AWARD   Shortlist

Smooth Naija King

Credits

Abena Annan, Isobar Nigeria, Client service

Smooth Naija King

Background

The smooth campaign was birthed in Nigeria, in collaboration with the global Budweiser team. it was aimed at celebrating the intrinsic qualities of the liquid. When the global assets were produced and tested in Nigeria, we identified 2 opportunities: To ladder from the functional to emotional benefits by including human elements and for additional personalisation for our different classes of consumers. To acheive this, we adapted the assets in 2 ways: One featured a dancer dancing to the smooth soundtrack and cameos from the brand's ambassadors and this targeted the younger 18 - 24 years demographic, while the other video featured the recently signed suave ex-BBN housemate Mike Edwards as he went to grab a bud with his friends (other BAs) after work and this was targeted at the older 25 - 34 years demographic. This was partnered with smooth kick-off NCP and smooth swap in-bar executions for a more holistic execution of the strategy.

Creative Idea

To launch the campaign we created two videos to this effect; one featured a dancer dancing to the smooth soundtrack and cameos from the brand's ambassadors, while the other video featured the brand recently signed suave ex-BBN housemate Mike Edwards, which juxtaposed his smooth mien with closeup shots of Budweiser's golden beer pouring and a pulsating soundtrack repeating the "smooth" phrase to create an unforgettable video that leaves the viewer with one thing;

Budweiser is smooth.

Strategy

Budweiser is proud of how its beer is brewed. Not only is it one of the few beers made from rice, the brand is also quick to let you know that it is the only beer brewed for 21 days making it one of the smoothest tasting beers.

However, this particular credential has not been established in most markets, so when we were tasked with creating the first Smooth campaign for Nigeria, we knew we had to emphasise this with our execution.

Execution

The radio ad also featured the same catchy soundtrack making sure anytime you heard the word "smooth" you thought of Budweiser.
Our out of home ads used the brand ambassadors with the same consistent message; "Budweiser is brewed smooth for Naija kings".
We created two videos to this effect; one featured a dancer dancing to the smooth soundtrack and cameos from the brand's ambassadors, while the other video featured the brand recently signed suave ex-BBN housemate Mike Edwards, which juxtaposed his smooth mien with closeup shots of Budweiser's golden beer pouring and a pulsating soundtrack repeating the "smooth" phrase to create an unforgettable video that leaves the viewer with one thing; Budweiser is smooth.

BRAND   Sonatel Orange Group
ENTRANT COMPANY Caractère, Dakar, Senegal
AWARD   Gold

JigeenJangale

Credits

Muriel Kla, Caractere, Executive Creative and Digital Director

Carole Bordes, Caractere, Copywriter

Alexandre Julienne, Caractere, Artistic director

Ernesto Hane, Caractere, Chief innovation Officer

Ali Diouf, Caractere, Head of strategy

Moussa Boye, Caractere, Media Manager

Mactar Diallo, Caractere, Social Media Manager

Arame Beye, Caractere, Community Manager

Ndeye Maguette Diawara, Caractere, Offline project Manager

Ndeye Rokhaya Diop, Caractere, Online project Manager

Ousmane Fall, Challenger, Producer

Gregory Ohrel, Challenger, Director

Seynabou Sarr, Caractere, Copywriter junior

Benedicte Samson, Caractere, Digital Factory Executive producer

JigeenJangale

Background

Sonatel Orange Group is the historical operator and leader in Senegal, also present in Mali, Guinea, Guinea Bissau and Sierra Leone. Although the group is very involved in the fields of education, the environment, culture and health through its foundation and its numerous CSR actions, its institutional image reflects its economic success rather than its societal commitment.

Creative Idea

Insight

Every year a girl stays at school, her future earnings increase between 10% to 20%.
In Senegal, girls outnumber boys and have better results at middle school. But at the University girls make only 40% of total student population due to various social barriers.

Challenge

Commit to keeping girls in school and make Sonatel Orange the Herald of this issue.

Creative idea

Engaging the community through emotion (Film fiction "On the way to school – Format 2mn et 4mn) and sharing experience (Social Experience) broadcasted only on digital). A platform (HumanInsideAfrica.com) that highlights the commitments of Sonatel Group and especially that for keeping girls in school through testimonies and true stories. #JigeenJangal (Girl Learn)

Strategy

We wanted to spark a large conversation around Girls education in the country. This issue needed to be addressed at scale if we wanted to have impact. The cultural context for women is particular in Senegal, many parents accept the idea of putting girls at school but few parents acknowledge the various barriers that hold them behind boys. We needed to show theses barriers and give a voice to women who struggled to have a proper education.

We targeted large public with a national TV spot and created testimonial contents of successful women who had to overcome many obstacles before succeeding. TV and Radio allowed us to reach large audiences and Digital helped us spread various contents (a social experience video, Testimonials, influencers posts, Stories and podcasts of successful women were developed).

Execution

The launch of the campaign took place on the eve of World Education Day with a TV platform sponsored by the brand dedicated to girls' education in Senegal. On this set the leaders of the group intervened. The emotional film "On the Way to School" was premiered, launching the conversation around #JigeenJangale. On D-Day (February 24, «World Education Day») the film was broadcast on TV and social

media with a call to action inviting people to visit the humaninsideafrica.com platform, listen to the podcasts and share their experiences as well. In radio, we also activated by broadcasting excerpts of podcasts testimonies inviting listeners to connect. On D+3 a series of stories were broadcast on Facebook and Instagram referring to the web platform. The conversation essentially focused on Twitter with an effective influence strategy.

On D+8 we then activated the second part. That of the experience with the broadcast of the film «testimonials» on our online channels.

Results

A positive, activist and action-oriented digital conversation hailed by all for its relevance and the emotion it generated, the #JiggeenJangal campaign generated an impressive stream of spontaneous testimonies. Young girls, women, but also fathers, brothers, or fellow students told of the barriers, the stops, the injustices, the broken dreams or, on the contrary, the paths of hope and pride that they experienced or crossed. These numerous testimonies opened the way to a change of mentality but also to proposals, Relationships or supportive and inspiring initiatives such as bringing highly educated women into schools to talk to young girls about trades and guidance, etc. The Jigeen Jangale campaign showed the Sonatel Orange group from a new perspective, sharing a unifying, modern and positive vision of society. Its willingness to accompany change with a strong voice was all the more perceived as it was legitimate in view of its long-standing support for girls' schooling, the digital inclusion of women and a gender-sensitive human resources policy. #JingeenJangal has federated speech and demonstrated that a societal and committed momentum can make things happen. As of March 30, 2020, the campaign reached more than 60% of the population in TV and radio and reached over: -6,200 mentions of the hashtag; -30,900 interactions; -132 Millions in digital of impressions.

How did Insight Enhance the Campaign?

The shocking statistics of women future earnings increasing between 10% to 20% every year they stay at school sounded as an alarm to raise awareness about the problem. Women earn far less in Senegal and lack of education is the major issue. Knowing that Insight we decided to make a bridge between the voices of successful women who had to fight to continue school and young girls who are actually experiencing these barriers.

While the TV spot showed the issue of the young girl, digital contents hosted in a dedicated platforms told the stories of successful women. The Social Experience reunited both narratives by melting the confident voices of successful women with the unsure voices of young girls at the surprise of their parents).

BRAND   NBC Universal
ENTRANT COMPANY Ogilvy Nigeria, Victoria Island, Nigeria
AWARD   Shortlist

Telemundo Africa Tik Tok Launch

Credits

Chidera Okehi, Ogilvy Nigeria, Social Media Manager

Topher Willis, NBC Universal, Client

Tik Tok Tik Tok, Social Media Manager, Collaborating company

Telemundo Africa Tik Tok Launch

Background
Telemundo Africa wanted to launch it's Tik-Tok channel in Africa and so to create awareness for the page, Telemundo Africa used the premiere of a brand new season of a super anticipated show, Iron Rose 2.

Creative Idea
The main character on the show Iron Rose, Altagracia Sandoval was a Boss lady who was super fashionable. She is not afraid to wear her heels, Red lipstick and the outfits that make her stand out even in a shootout scene. We told fans to rub their red lipstick like the Boss lady will while dancing to the song chosen for the campaign - Say Cheese by Kidi Music.

Strategy
Our Target audience was Passionistas aged 25 - 35 who have TikTok accounts and want more from the Brand. The Target media used was TikTok. The plan included use of Heavy TikTok female influencers from all over Africa. We used Talents (actors from Iron Rose) Kika Edgar, Aracely Arambula and a few Passionistas to create the first set of videos to show fans in a promo video what we expect from them.

Execution
The campaign was executed with Influencers around Africa, most of which were Nigerians to suit our priority TA - Lily Afe, Laura Ikeji, Juliet Ibrahim, Iyabo Ojo etc. Kidi Music's song titled Say Cheese was used include our Ghanaian audience. We ran the campaign from June - August and different assets were used to push promotions at different stages. Promo Videos, Placement ads on header and page takeover on the TikTok app. Instagram and Facebook assets to cross promote the campaign and create awareness.

Results
The campaign hashtag #IronRoseChallenge was used over 2.5m times and Telemundo gained over 4,000 new fans on TikTok.
Passionistas took part in the challenge even the fans that are not on TikTok took part in the competition around other social media platforms.

How did Insight Enhance the Campaign?
We recognised our audience like to see themselves in the stars. They love to feel like a part of the show and participate in whatever the brand is working on. They also love when the brand Telemundo is localised for them.
By using a known nuance from the main character (Her red lipstick) made the fans see them selves in the Talent.
They love that if they are on TikTok, they can interact with the brand on that platform as well.
They love that they saw local celebrities participate in the challenge, they saw that Passionistas like them were used to promote the challenge as well.
Fans also appreciated the brand went further to use a familiar sound from a familiar national musician.

BRAND	Guinness Ghana (A Diageo Company)
ENTRANT COMPANY	mediaReach OMD, Accra, Ghana
AWARD	Bronze

My Malta Guinness Story

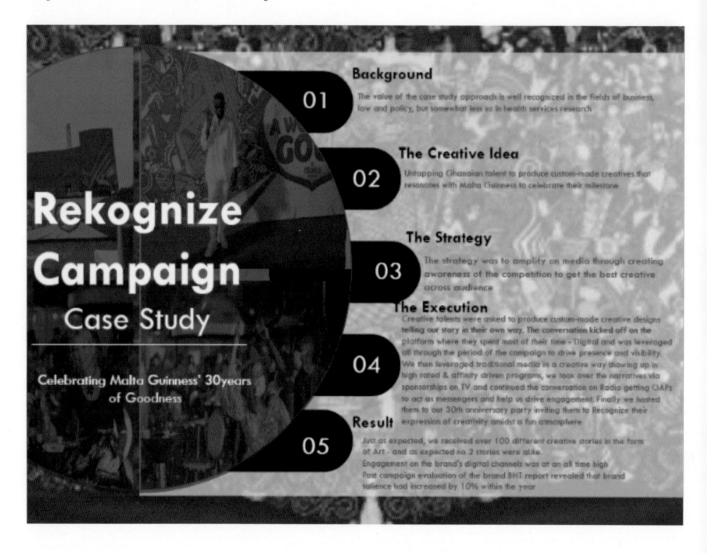

Credits

Gideon Quaku, OMD, Team Lead

Justina Korley, OMD, Planner

Magdaline Afutu, PHD, Planner

Taniya Mondal, OMD, Account Director

David Ofosuhene, OMD, Head of Strategy

My Malta Guinness Story

Background
The Malta Guinness brand which has been 30 years in the market had had some level of success in Ghana.

However, seeing the level of disruption in the marketing space and consumer habits in recent times, it was important to have a complete rethink of how we approached marketing and consumer engagement. The challenge for the brand was how to engage the actively mobile and radical youths in Ghana in a way that had meaning for them and at the same time drive salience for the brand.

Creative Idea
We realized that the average Ghanaian youth is bursting with creative energy constantly seeking expression and appreciation. We decided to create a platform for this expression by directly asking the talents to showcase what they have got no holds barred.

Strategy
Our 30th anniversary was the perfect opportunity to do this rather than try to tell our story our way like we have always done, we flipped the script and asked for their honest opinion asking them to tell us the Malta Guinness story from their own perspective. This move will be the beginning of a new level of engagement with this energetic target group

Execution
Creative talents were asked to produce custom-made creative designs telling our story in their own way.
The conversation kicked off on the platform where they spent most of their time - Digital and was leveraged all through the period of the campaign to drive presence and visibility. We then leveraged traditional media in a creative way showing up in high rated & affinity driven programs, we took over the narratives via sponsorships on TV and continued the conversation on Radio getting OAPs to act as messengers and help us drive engagement.

Finally we hosted them to our 30th anniversary party inviting them to Recognize their expression of creativity amidst a fun atmosphere.

Results
Just as expected, we received over 100 different creative stories in the form of Art - and as expected no 2 stories were alike.

Engagement on the brand's digital channels was at an all time high post campaign evaluation of the brand BHT report revealed that brand salience had increased by 10% within the year.

How did Insight Enhance the Campaign?
An understanding of the psychography of the TG was essential to the winning idea rather than try to tell our story our way like we have always done, we flipped the script and asked for their honest opinion asking them to tell us the Malta Guinness story from their own perspective.

Use of **Media**

BRAND   Henkel
ENTRANT COMPANY   mediaReach OMD, Lagos, Nigeria
AWARD   Bronze

WAW Moments on BBN

Credits

Ngozi Uwafili, mediareach OMD, Media Planner

WAW Moments on BBN

Background

The brand Waw was launched in the media space in 2019 to compete against the big players like the likes of So Klin, Sunlight, Ariel etc. Budget was a major constraint and given the fact again that 2020 was an exceptional year because of the impact of COVID-19 across the world including Nigeria in terms of reduction in products demand across all categories amongst consumers globally. We needed to find a smart way to connect with the consumers and deliver on ROI at very optimal cost whilst growing traction, consideration, and adoption for the brand- Waw.

Creative Idea

The idea was for us to own the Word Waw as in Wao!!... Wao is supposed to be synonymous with expression of some awesome experience so owing that cliché within an environment or ambiance where our TG connects with would aid to drive TOMA, recall and ultimately brand consideration. So, we played around Wao but as in "Waw". We built the whole concept around "Waw Moments"

Strategy

There are lots of detergent within the soap and detergent market space- so we needed to call out our brand USP - Waw treats colured clothes nicely unlike other detergent that would most times deface colours in clothes overtime- Insights from consumer perspective is that they would readily embrace detergent that would take care of their precious-coloured fabrics. It was imperative for us to tie this key attribute via our ``Waw Moments`` concept with target group through several tactical executions.

Execution

Full participation in 2020 BBN and built our presence on our thematic model- ``Waw Moments`` through the following executions within the house-

1.Product Integration: We owned the laundry space with Henkel products & branded inventory to drive visibility on screen.
2.Task Sponsorship: Got housemates in two competitions to showcase the key brand benefits of WAW.
3.Branding & Customization: The housemates wore branded outfits on both task days. The winning teams were handed prizes and all participants received a year supply of Henkel products.

Results

Full participation in 2020 BBN and built our presence on our thematic model- ``Waw Moments`` through the following executions within the house-
1.Product Integration: We owned the laundry space with Henkel products & branded inventory to drive visibility on screen.
2.Task Sponsorship: Got housemates in two competitions to showcase the key brand benefits of WAW.
3.Branding & Customization: The housemates wore branded outfits on both task days. The winning teams were handed prizes and all participants received a year supply of Henkel products.

BRAND   UAC- CAP PLC
ENTRANT COMPANY   mediaReach OMD, Maryland,Lagos, Nigeria
AWARD   Bronze

Dulux BBN 2020

Credits

Ngozi Uwafili, mediareach OMD, Media Planner

Dulux BBN 2020

Background

Dulux Paints has been in the paint industry for over 20 years following a series of name changes in the early 1990s. With an exhaustive array of paint colors and paint types, Dulux paints is yet to attain the expected level of awareness among it's Target Audience. With the objective to increase awareness and sales, we leveraged the biggest TV show, Big Brother 2020, lockdown edition.

Creative Idea

To drive awareness for Dulux paints through the USP of VALUE "Do more with Less" and showcase the array of Dulux Paint colors through brand association with Nigeria's Biggest TV Entertainment Show (BBN 2020)

Strategy

Use of paint has gone beyond regular painting. Majority of consumers are looking to apply paint that brings to life a particular design or space, they are also cost conscious and are looking to use paint that is cost effective yet can deliver extensive coverage on large areas. To communicate the "Value for Less" of Dulux paints, we used the visual imagery of TV to show the brand in-use.

Execution

Dulux paints were exclusively used to paint the house where the show's contestant lived in for 3 months. This provided round-the-clock visibility for the brand on the 24-hour reality show and showcased the wide array of Dulux Colors in use in creative ways.

In the Dulux-sponsored Tasks, the housemates were grouped in 2 Teams and challenged to create a Mood Board based on the brief. The brief presented 2 different room setting having varying functionalities. A dulux shop was placed nearby for Housemates to select the best fit Colours based on the functionality of the room.

The teams were judged on Colour coordination, Creativity, Presentation and Quantity of paint used. This Task idea was aimed at showcasing the ability of Dulux Paint to deliver on the desired design, style and decor taste whilst showing how a little amount of paint delivers desired results. This was broadcast on TV; online platforms (Twitter, Instagram & Facebook) were also leveraged to drive the conversation.

Results

1. There was a significant increase across online platforms with immense online traction, engagement and followership for Dulux Paint.

2. Increased website traffic by 15%

3. Increase in sales of Dulux paints

BRAND   GODREJ NIGERIA LIMITED
ENTRANT COMPANY   mediaReach OMD, Maryland, Lagos, Nigeria
AWARD   Bronze

Darling Hair BBN

Credits

Titi Adebayo, mediaReach OMD, Media Buyer

Darling Hair BBN

Background

The country had been on a total lockdown for 3 months prior and this had caused a downturn in the sales of Darling Hair products in the markets as there was no motivation for people to make their hair at all, it was also impossible considering that beauty parlors were locked down based on the strong directives form the government to help curb the virus. As many people all over the world began to try out new things to keep busy, Nigerian women had no choice but to go the Do-It-Yourself route as regards beauty and personal grooming; this birthed the need for Darling Hair to encourage creative and individual use of her products.

Creative Idea

Many of the brand's target audience were already spending a lot of time on audio-visual platforms in a bid to learn and practice styling their hair by themselves.TV viewership had also increased massively during the pandemic and the popular reality TV show, Big Brother Naija was scheduled to return to screen in that time, we saw an opportunity to connect our products with the needs of consumers by bringing DIY footages to a bigger audience than Youtube.

Strategy

Targeting women between 18-45 years in the Social Economic Class B and C who are stylish and fashion progressive, it is important that we presented as a brand that understood her pain as the pandemic and lockdown were concerned. No aspect of life was business as usual and that included her beauty routines and personal grooming so we leveraged TV to communicate that we are with her through the times by adopting the DIY route at the Big Brother Naija Lockdown Edition. Instead of having professional hairstylists make the hair of the housemates, video footages were instead shown to the housemates detailing a step by step method of achieving popular hairdos.

Execution

Beyond running our TVC that amplified our theme and connected audience at high frequency, we had the Darling hair Exclusive salon open every Sunday morning to all housemates on the show to style their hair by themselves. Video clips were shown in the salon to demonstrate how to make different hairstyles. Because making one's hair by oneself is not an easy feat, we knew we had to encourage weekly participation from the housemates through incentives. They were scored on creativity and maintenance and the housemate with the overall score at the end of the season won the sum of 2M NGN. On one of the days in the house, we also tasked the housemates to showcase their creativity in a runway fashion show as well as a vogue-inspired photoshoot. They were asked to create "Africa themed hair styles" on one another and showcase these using props and costumes provided.

Results

1. The task had our hashtag "DarlinghairXBBN" trending on twitter all day with a lot of conversations generated by the viewers at home.
2. We launched the Darling Empress collection (human hair) and all our products were sold out within the first month of Launch.
3. 20% increase in our followers across all social media platforms.
4. Launched the online shopping and home delivery platform and this has resulted in the double size of sales of out products.

BRAND   Caraway Foods International Nigeria
ENTRANT COMPANY   mediaReach OMD, Maryland, Lagos, Nigeria
AWARD   Bronze

Tasty Tom

Credits

Titi Adebayo, mediaReach OMD, Media Buyer

Ebere Ejidike, Olam Nigeria, Caraway Foods International Nigeria

Tasty Tom

Background
Due to NBC Ban on the advertisement of tomato paste in Nigeria, Tasty Tom has not been able to run communication Campaigns for their Brand. They have been in the market for years without being able to create awareness for the Brand hence the need for alternative use of media to generate awareness for the brand

Creative Idea
Irrespective of government clamp downs, the tomato paste category is superfluous with numerous brands but only a few are top of mind. A subliminal integrative campaign "Cooking made Easy with Tasty Tom!" was conceived to bring to limelight the dishes and delicacies that can be achieved using Tasty Tom jollof paste and pepper mix.

Strategy
Chefs have become celebrities to food lovers and a lot of our target audience look up to this them for cooking inspirations and product recommendation so we encouraged them to infuse our products in their meals with the objective of increasing of our products. Also, due to the current Pandemic situation in the country, we discovered a lot of target audience have shown interest in learning how to prepare different food by watching cooking shows on TV and browsing about them online.

We took advantage of this opportunity by doing a subtle integration with popular cooking shows on TV, whereby the presenters/chefs are given our products to come up with different dishes and prepare on TV.

Execution
We identified Top rated Cookery Programs that have National reach and affinity with our Target Audience to associate with

We integrated all our 3 brands into the different programs. We had Tasty tom Tomato paste, The jollof Mix and the Tasty Tom Noodles. The chefs came up with different interesting dishes they could prepare with each our products. Since these shows were prerecorded, we subliminally infused our products into the hosts choice of dish and ensured that the brand was amplified albeit suggestively.

The show was deployed across TV and cascaded to the social media platform such as Facebook and Instagram and we also had people share this contents on their own social media pages of the chefs.

BRAND Tolaram Group

ENTRANT COMPANY mediaReach OMD, Maryland, Lagos, Nigeria

AWARD Bronze

Wipe off COVID with Hypo

Credits

Oluwabukola Bankole, Tolaram Group, Media Buying Manager

Akintayo Akinseloyin, Tolaram Group, Brand Manager

Emmanuel Adediran, mediaReach OMD, Lead Strategist

Jubilee Okuwe mediaReach OMD, Media Buyer

Precious Adeleye, mediaReach OMD, Media Planner

Wipe off COVID with Hypo

Background

Hypo bleach is one of Nigeria's most successful brands, having dominated the bleach category with over 95% market share in less than 4 years after launch, the objective for this year was to grow by 50%. One of the challenges the brand faced is that consumers only relate to the whitening property of bleach and only use it for laundry of white fabrics. The objective was to grow by increasing usage occasions among consumers

Creative Idea

When COVID hit the country, the brand decided to seize the opportunity to change consumer perception and drive association for bleach as a disinfectant. We had 2 major factors to our advantage. The WHO listed bleach as a disinfectant in its COVID 19 guideline (We know the populace relied almost entirely on trusted sources like the CDC and WHO for information about the virus and quickly adopted all recommendations). Competition (sanitizers & disinfectants) was overpriced and in limited supply because of demand surge; we were the perfect alternative priced at N20 a sachet & readily available

Strategy

The strategy was to leverage the COVID situation to drive a new association for the brand as a disinfectant not just a whitener. We aimed to Re-introduce Hypo bleach as more than a whitener but also the most affordable disinfectant potent to protect they and their loved ones against the deadly COVID. We leveraged the credibility of the WHO to drive this new association knowing that our TG would easily be influenced to use bleach as the disinfectant seeing it was recommended by the reputable organization. Visual media channel were key to help demonstrate the product in use and also emphasize the properties hence channels like OOH, TV & digital were considered. We would also use influencers to show them how to use the product in this new light

Execution

We had the campaign in three phases, Tell, Show and Convert.

First, the brand launched a high impact integrated campaign across traditional and social media platforms, the objective was to sensitize the public on the deadly virus and position Hypo as the cheapest way to fight the virus citing the WHO recommendation. During the lockdown, seeing the shift in media habits, we suspended OOH & Press but increased TV & Digital. We resorted to a different narrative which was an infomercial 'Wipe off COVID; Disinfect your home with hypo'' where we focused on showing the product in use and demonstrating the disinfecting properties via TV & Social media. Leveraging heavily on News (because of the increased interest in COVID updates) and use of influencers we showed how the product could be used in surface and household cleaning, the focus for TV was on grassroot penetration across all affected markets.

Results

From a post campaign survey, we reached over 100m Nigerians and our Ad recall was 90% exceeding that of other popular disinfectants like Dettol. From sales report, rather than a decline in a time when consumption could have declined, sales of Hypo for the campaign period increased by over 86%. We were able to get 40% attribution in 3 months. This campaign made it easy for consumers to see, know and accept Hypo Bleach as more than a Fabric Whitener but also an affordable disinfectant.

BRAND   Tolaram Group

ENTRANT COMPANY   mediaReach OMD, Maryland, Lagos, Nigeria

AWARD   Silver

Indomie Owambe Party

Credits

Oluwabukola Bankole, Tolaram Group, Media Buying Manager

Aramide Ayeni, DUFIL Prima, Media Manager

Yinka Adebayo, OMG WeCA, ED, Media Investments & Sponsorship

Doris Ohanugo, Multichoice Nigeria, Senior Sales Manager

Emmanuel Adediran, mediaReach OMD, Lead Strategist

Adedoyin Aladesanmi, mediaReach OMD, Media Buyer

Indomie Owambe Party

Background

Following the advent of COVID 19 in Nigeria, the country went on total lockdown with restrictions of public gatherings which left Nigerians longing for their weekend fun times. In response to the pandemic, most brands switched from thematic advertising and flooded the airwaves with COVID related messages; it was monotonous, boring and predictable. We needed an innovative way to cut through the clutter.

Our approach was to create meaningful experiences that connect with the needs of our consumers in a brand-safe way while staying sensitive to the situation at hand.

Creative Idea

We gathered that consumers were constantly looking to alternative means of entertainment to distract themselves from the fear-laden COVID messages.

Our idea was informed by insights pointing to what consumers missed the most during the lockdown – weekend parties & social moments outdoor. We sought to leverage nostalgia and bring Nigerian families a taste of the long missed fun moments from weekend parties while staying safe in the comfort of their homes. Nigerians love to party during the weekends, they attend weddings, naming ceremonies and the likes. One thing that is common to all these parties are Live Bands. This led to the big idea "Owanbe Saturday" where live bands will perform Live on TV to give people the experience they are missing due to the lockdown.

Strategy

The strategy was to leverage the reach of linear TV and drive massive engagement on social media to achieve our objectives. We also leveraged the power of influencer marketing to build quick awareness and followership by getting the popular celebrities to create skits to build anticipation towards their performance on the show. We partnered with the foremost entertainment channel – DSTV for pan Nigeria reach and featured some of the most popular Musicians & comedians in a 3 hour live performance of Naija music & comedy suitable for the family.

Execution

Pre Event, we announced via massive promotion on TV & digital platforms; The artistes and comedians were also tasked to promote the show via video skits to drive their audience to watch the show on Saturday. The biggest virtual stage in Nigeria was set and the audience were treated every Saturday night to live performance on TV from the comfort of their homes. In order to drive engagement on digital, we introduced segments into the show featuring performances from the most popular artists & comedians who added fun and laughter to the show On the Day of the show, viewers were asked to send videos of themselves dancing to the music for a chance to get streamed live on the show; To sustain the conversation on social during the week we asked viewers to cook their favourite Indomie noodles creatively and post on their handles tagging the brand, we also asked them to guess the name of the next celebrity performance will be; winners from these competitions won a year supply of Indomie,

Results

The Indomie Owambe show grew in popularity recording a 330% increase in viewership and over 320m in social reach. Consumer engagement were highest for the brand with over 22.9m posts and over 20,000 entries weekly, the #AMOwambe trended every Saturday. Owambe trended no. 1 every Saturday all through the period of the show. Due to the prolonged lockdown, most of the celebrities had been out of business for so long, so when the opportunity to perform presented itself with Pan Nigeria exposure they jumped at it and all agreed to perform free of charge. The video skits were also produced free of cost. By this, we were able to get earned media worth 15m free of cost for the brand and created a win-win partnership for both our brand and the celebrities. Sales of the brand super pack SKU also increased by 35% during the period of the show

BRAND   Budweiser
ENTRANT COMPANY   Isobar, Ikeja, Nigeria
AWARD   Bronze

Smooth Kick-Off

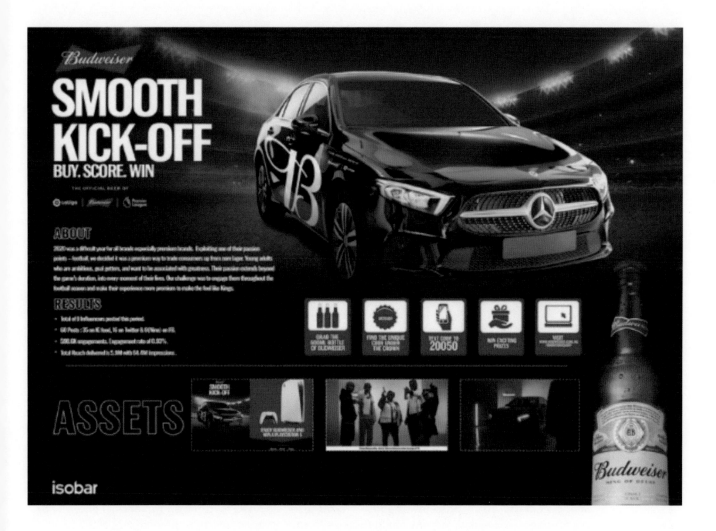

Credits

Abena Annan, Isobar Nigeria, Senior Group head, Client service

Smooth Kick-Off

Background
2020 was a tough year for all brands especially premium brands. We decided that land football was a premium way to trade consumers up from core lager.

Creative Idea
For Budweiser to position itself as premium beer for premium football occasions, energized by the sounds of the game.

Relying on one of our passion points which is football, we infused a premium experience into it by celebrating the greatness of the players on and off the pitch.

Strategy
Young adults who are ambitious, goal getters, and want to be associated with greatness. Their passion extends beyond the game's duration, into every moment of their lives.

Our strategy is to engage them throughout the football season and make their experience even more interesting.

Execution
- Begin association with the league by creating excitement that drives conversation.
- Announce our presence with a bang, through digital experiences that disrupt existing behaviour & create regular engagement.
- Keep the momentum going but leveraging consumer excitement through rewards.

Results
At the end of the campaign 1 lucky TA won a Mustang Overall throughout the Smooth Thematic Campaign we had:
- Total of 9 Influencers posted this period.
- 60 Posts : 35 on IG feed, 16 on Twitter & 9(Nine) on FB
- 598.6K engagements. Engagement rate of 0.93%
- Total Reach delivered is 5.9M with 64.4M impressions

BRAND   Flutterwave

ENTRANT COMPANY   mediaReach OMD, Maryland, Lagos, Nigeria

AWARD   Shortlist

Secured Satisfaction

Credits

Olugbenga Agboola, Flutterwave, CEO/Co-Founder

Yewande Akomolafe-Kalu, Flutterwave, Chief Storyteller

Omosola Aworinde, mediaReach OMD, Account Manager/Client Service

Secured Satisfaction

Background

Flutterwave for business is an online payment platform that brings SMES and big organization to the full glare of their customer. Providing the customer with a more flexible means of making and receiving payment.

Having existed for three years, the brand suffered public perception owing to significant low level of awareness and audience understanding of the business offering.

The story soon changed when the business was introduced to best practice integrated marketing.

Creative Idea

To better understand the how to shape perception and win audience trust, further consumer understanding was required.

It was gathered from the data analysis that there were 2 major buckets of the TG needed to be reached differently.

1. The Young and dynamic
2. Business Executives

A deep dive revealed that the young audience will love flexibility and convenience while the Business Executive is keen on Security.

To connect with the two categories of audience, their passion points became to focus and a reliable tool to reach both categories; showing that Flutterwave have all it will takes to give them seamless and secured online payment transaction which will in turn grow their businesses.

Strategy

The single-minded proposition was to leverage on a platform with high followership where a huge percentage of our core audience consumes.

Focus was geared toward program with high affinity on platform that resonate with the product offering. Deployed Cable TV to reach the larger part of the audience. Since trust and security was to be won, attention was targeted at sponsorship to spur consumer engagement.

Execution

On TV, spots execution was placed within Business news both on Cable & Terrestrial platforms to connect with Business Executives while Entertainment, Movies & Musical content were targeted to reach the young audience.

Tactical interviews were also deployed to enable brand owners call out the USP of the brand within top-rated talk shows.

On Radio, we also drove engagement with live appearance where brand managers were able to answer key questions to enlighten the audience.

We also amplified the videos and drove engagement online to show trend and relevance.

Digital

The online platform actively focused on wide reach to drive awareness across board. Rated trust contents on socials with organic growth and Programmatic buy to drive incremental reach.

Results

Post campaign evaluation from client shows a significant increase in overall business objectives and also surpassed expectation.

The awareness level increased such that client recorded 125% increase in new business sign-ups at the end of August.

BRAND   Ministry of Maritime Economy of Cape Verde.

ENTRANT COMPANY   Mantra Pu, Praia, Cape Verde

AWARD   Bronze

Fisherman

Credits

Júnior Lisboa, Mantra, Creative Director

Júnior Lisboa, Mantra, Copywriter

André Ferraz, Art Director

Fisherman

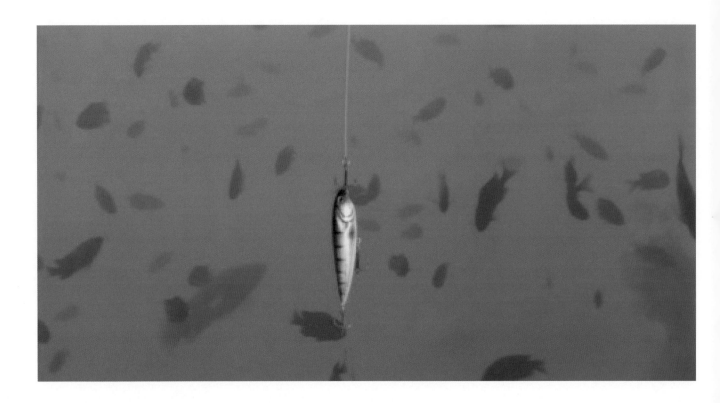

Background
Fisherman's Day, celebrated on February 5, is an important date in the calendar of actions of the Ministry of Maritime Economy of Cape Verde.

Creative Idea
The idea was to show how deep a fisherman can go to make a living. Using Facebook's Canvas tool, we initially showed only one line in the water and an invitation to people to slide across the screen of the phone until they found the message, over the bottom of the ocean - in fact, a hook with a bait. The text announced: To those go so far for their living, deserves all of our support.

Strategy
To mark a position with fishermen and opinion leaders, the agency created a mobile action to Facebook hosted in Ministry of Maritime Economy of Cape Verde's page

Execution
Using Facebook's Canvas tool, we initially showed only one line in the water and an invitation to people to slide across the screen of the phone until they found the message, over the bottom of the ocean.

Results
The action had a large number of interactions and helped the Ministry to make a stand with the initially determined target audience.

BRAND   Guinness Ghana Brewery Limited
ENTRANT COMPANY   mediaReach OMD, Accra, Ghana
AWARD   Bronze

Rekognize Campaign

Rekognize Campaign
Case Study

Celebrating Malta Guinness' 30years
of Goodness

01 Background
The value of the case study approach is well recognized in the fields of business, law and policy, but somewhat less so in health services research

02 The Creative Idea
Untapping Ghanaian talent to produce custom-made creatives that resonates with Malta Guinness to celebrate their milestone

03 The Strategy
The strategy was to amplify on media through creating awareness of the competition to get the best creative across audience

04 The Execution
Creative talents were asked to produce custom-made creative designs telling our story in their own way. The conversation kicked off on the platform where they spent most of their time - Digital and was leveraged all through the period of the campaign to drive presence and visibility. We then leveraged traditional media in a creative way showing up in high rated & affinity driven programs, we took over the narratives via sponsorships on TV and continued the conversation on Radio getting OAPs to act as messengers and help us drive engagement. Finally we hosted them to our 30th anniversary party inviting them to Recognize their expression of creativity amidst a fun atmosphere

05 Result
Just as expected, we received over 100 different creative stories in the form of Art - and as expected no 2 stories were alike.
Engagement on the brand's digital channels was at an all time high
Post campaign evaluation of the brand BHT report revealed that brand salience had increased by 10% within the year

Credits

Gideon Quaku, OMD, Manager

Rekognize Campaign

Background
This campaign was setup as part of the brand's 30th anniversary. It came with a challenge to find a new packaging design for the anniversary and was done to champion a 'can-do' attitude, by positioning MG as a supporter of local creativity.

Creative Idea
The Ghanaian is full of untapped skill & natural abilities. Some of which when properly engaged can boost brand building. Diageo sort to give an opportunity to the Ghanaian people to unearth their hidden abilities and Malta Guinness being a brand cutting across generations, leveraged on media to drive awareness of this creativity of people to come up with a limited edition label to celebrate the 30th anniversary of a prestigious brand.

Strategy
The core strategy was invite talented Ghanaians to come up with bespoke design to mark the 30th anniversary of the brand. We had to use media to create awareness amongst artists to come up with the best design. The design would be out doored and rolled out on every bottle label during the period.

Execution
Digital was used to maintain & boost online presence and visibility. Artists were then encouraged to submit their best designs to generate the excitement for the brand. We leverage on traditional media and Played on high rated & affinity driven programs, supporting sponsorships on TV to drive frequency and meaningfulness. on Radio to drill down messaging & comprehension. the used hypes by dedicated and influential radio presenters were used as campaign influencers to drive incremental reach and engagement.

Results
Campaign delivered 79.54% reach and received 100+ entries of new designs for their 30th anniversary.

Credits

Gideon Quaku, OMD, Manager

BRAND   Pick n Eat Ltd (KFC local franchiser)
ENTRANT COMPANY   CIRCUS! Mauritius, Moka, Mauritius
AWARD   Gold

KFC Say No To Plastic

Credits

Vincent Montocchio, CIRCUS!, Executive Creative Director

Fabrice Thevenet, CIRCUS!, Creative Director

Melissa Veerapen, CIRCUS!, Art Director

Lara Marot, CIRCUS!, Client Service Director

Jean Christophe Ah Seng, CIRCUS!, Production Manager

KFC Say No To Plastic

Background
KFC is one of the biggest users of plastic straws in the world. In Mauritius, the figures are as alarming even though we are a very small island. KFC wanted to change that by saying no to plastic straws.

Creative Idea
KFC decided to make a drastic change by categorically saying no to these plastic straws. Since the figures of wasted straws thrown into nature both worldwide and locally are frightening enough, we decided to show the wastage literally using numbers and facts.

Strategy
Because no one realises how much straws are actually used and thrown in a day, in a week or in a month, we literally showed how much of these plastic straws are used with a bold message and shocking figures to make a powerful and lasting impact.

Execution
From the 21 KFC stores across Mauritius, 40 000 used straws were collected over a month. These were then placed in specially made billboards to show how much are used and thrown.

Results
The whole initiative was highly lauded on social media and the press while KFC was described as an example to follow by other fast food outlets.

BRAND   True Blue Development - Kimpton Kawana Bay

ENTRANT COMPANY   Nelson Reids, Lagos, Nigeria

AWARD   Bronze

Kimpton Kawana Bay

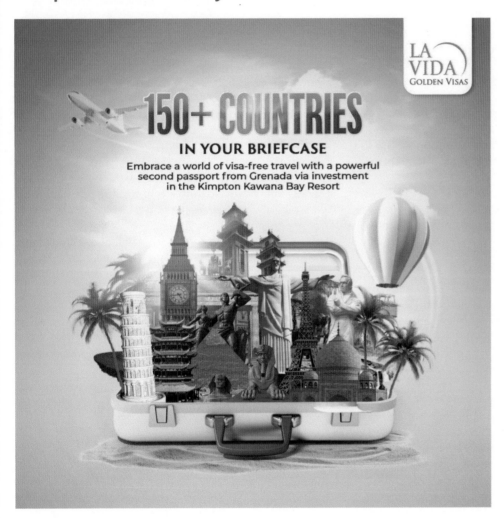

Credits

Ikechukwu Maduka, Nelson Reids, Strategy

Kareem Kayode, Nelson Reids, Design

Stephen Umezurike, Nelson Reids, Strategy

Izu Bielonwu, Nelson Reids, Marketing

Chidi Adenekan, Nelson Reids, Accounts

ify Aralu, Nelson Reids, Digital Lead

Obafemi Thanni, Nelson Reids, Creative Writer

Kimpton Kawana Bay

Background

Developers of Grenada's most elite Citizenship by Investment Project, True Blue Development, and Internationally renowned Investment Migration Firm, La Vida Golden Visas, hired Nelson Reids to attract High Net Worth Individuals to purchase its $250,000 title-deeded suits and studios, in exchange for Grenadian Citizenship and its benefits which include Visa-Free Travel to the 150+ countries.

Nelson Reids was tasked with the following responsibilities:

1. Create awareness amongst the Nigerian HNWI community.
2. Educate the Nigerian HNWI community on the limitations of the Nigerian passport and the need for visa-free travel.
3. Establish Kimpton Kawana Bay as the most elite Citizenship By Investment Project in the Carribeans.
4. Wrestle attention and share of mind from key competitors, Range Developments.
5. Generate high-quality leads.

Creative Idea

To get Nigerian HNWIs to make a N103m ($250,000) buying decision, we needed to find the right balance between rationality and emotion. We needed to show the value of our clients offering from a financial and business standpoint whilst also playing to their vanity and ego.

1. "What's the whole point of being rich if you still travel like Aunty Ruka from Isale Eko?" - An approach appealing to their vanity, ego and logic.
2. "150+ countries in your briefcase" demonstrating the power of the Grenada passport and its visa-free access to the EU, China, Singapore, Russia and 150 others.
3. "Kimpton Kawana Bay and the $17m opportunity for African Investors" and "This piece of real estate offers African Investors the key to Global Domination" - An insightful approach showing the extra benefits of the Kawana. Bay CBI project.
4. "Wealthy African, How Valuable is your passport", "Choosing the right Citizenship By Investment Program" - An educational approach

Strategy

We conducted a deep dive into the personality and behaviors of the Nigerian HNWI community. We identified how they consume digital information and identified four instrumental digital media platforms they rely on for business, finance and investing information: BusinessDay, Nairametrics and Forbes. We also selected ThisDay as it is the only newspaper placed at the EAN private jet terminal where Lagos-based HNWIs often fly out from.

We used a combination of the Nigerian Stock Exchange, Bloomberg and High Society club memberships to identify and produce a list of 300 HNWIs in Nigeria. A further deep dive showed that around 55% had active LinkedIn Profiles. This would set the tone for execution of our campaign.

Execution

A. Every two weeks, we launched a series of high-level articles, interviews, editorials and display ads across our select digital and print media and television programmes, including Forbes, BusinessDay, AIT, BBC Africa, Nairametrics, ThisDay, Vanguard, TheNation and others.
B. We uploaded our list of HNWIs into Linkedin's custom-audience feature to reach over 55% of our target audience directly with our banner, editorials, interviews and articles and invites to an exclusive webinar.
C. Created and aired a television documentary as well as an exclusive Interview
D. Orchestrated and moderated an exclusive webinar with 52 HNWI attendees.
E. Created a brochure shaped as a replica Grenada passport and handed it to wealthy Nigerian customers at Caribbean restaurants in Lagos.

Results

Agency Results

-Increased Nigerian applications and sales of the Kawana Bay by 300% in 6 months. Contributing to over 7 million dollars ($7m) in sales from Nigeria alone in the last 6 months.
-Ranked Number 1 on Google Nigeria for how to get a second passport.

Shared Results

- In Q1 and Q2, Kawana Bay accounted for 57% of all real estate CBI investment.

BRAND   Diageo Ghana

ENTRANT COMPANY   mediaReach OMD, Accra, Ghana

AWARD   Silver

Johnnie Walker 200th Anniversary

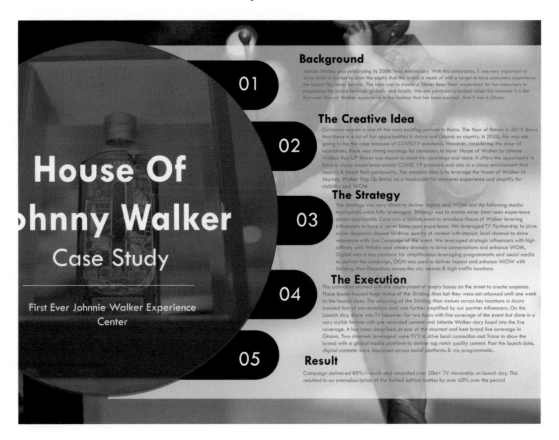

Credits

Emmanuel Amankwah, Now Available Africa, Creative Director

Yvonne Acheampong, Now Available Africa, Client Service Director

Venus Tawiah, Now Available Africa, Director, Business and Communications

Anna Agostinelli, Now Available Africa, Account Manager

Shaaibatu Abdul Rasheed, Now Available Africa, Social Media and Influencer Executive

Samira Saadu, Now Available Africa, Account Manager

Whitney Dena Thompson, Now Available Africa, Senior Social Media Manager

Christina Ogoussan, Now Available Africa, Social Media Manager

Emeka Dele, Now Available Africa, Media Strategist

Akwesi Wiredu Agyekum, Now Available Africa, Motion Graphics and Design

Johnnie Walker 200th Anniversary

Background

As part of the 200th anniversary of the brand Johnny Walker in Ghana, it was very important to drive scale in market to show the equity that the brand is made of with a target to have consumers experience the brand like never before..

The media objective was to create massive impact demonstrating creativity at its peak in a manner that will guarantee consumer engagement and conversations beyond the time of year

Creative Idea

The idea was to create a 'Never Been Seen' experience for our consumers to emphasize the brand heritage globally and locally. We were going to deliver impact by using media in a way not done before in our market.

Strategy

The strategy was to use an interplay of ATL channels and experiential (BTL) to tell the brand story in a manner that captivates Ghanaians and gets them talking all through the campaign period and beyond. We were deliberate to select online and offline media channels that will deliver on our impact objectives and seamlessly integrates with the BTL plans. For offline, OOH and TV were prioritized to drive reach & awareness.

While digital was deployed to extend reach and drive conversations among TA around the experience curated at the House of Walker center; we employed social media & influencer marketing to drive conversations and enhance WOM, programmatic buying ensured our targeting was optimal and extremely efficient.
For BTL : Our House of Walker was designed to create the memorable experiences that matched the anticipation we had built using other ATL media channels

Execution

The activation started with the deployment of empty boxes on the street to create suspense.
These boxes housed mega-sized statue of the Signature Johnie Walker figurine - "The Striding Man" but they were not unboxed until one week to the launch date.

The unboxing of the Striding Man statues across key locations in Accra created lots of conversations and was further amplified by our partner influencers. On the Launch day, there was TV takeover for two hours with live coverage of the event but done in a very stylish format with pre recorded content and Johnnie Walker story fused into the live coverage. It has been described as one of the smartest and best brand live coverage in Ghana. Two channels leveraged were TV3 to drive local connection and Trace to show the brand with a global media platform to deliver top notch quality content. Post the launch date, digital contents were deployed across social platforms & via programmatic.
Nothing like this has happened in Ghana before.

Results

We were the talk of Ghana all through the campaign
Campaign delivered 88%+ reach and recorded over 20m+ TV viewership on launch day. This resulted in an oversubscription of the limited edition bottles by over 60% over the period
We trended week on week and did achieve our objective of creating a memorable experience for our TA

Credits

Audrey Quaye, Now Available Africa, Graphic Designer

Frank Otu Now Available Africa Art Director

Selase Fiakpui, Now Available Africa, Copywriter

Isaac Fuseini, Now Available Africa, Production Manager

Constance Afua Mensah, Now Available Africa, Traffic Manager

Lesego Lesbogang Mohale, Guinness Ghana Breweries PLC (Diageo), Portfolio Marketing Manager

Abena Chrappah, Guinness Ghana Breweries PLC (Diageo), Digital and Media Manager

Wilma Amoo-Osae, Guinness Ghana Breweries PLC (Diageo), Assistant Brand Manager

Abdul-Samed Sadiq, Guinness Ghana Breweries PLC (Diageo), Senior Brand Manager (Spirits)

BRAND   ACPL Ghana
ENTRANT COMPANY mediaReach OMD, Accra, Ghana
AWARD   Shortlist

A-Life Soap Campaign

01

Background

During the COVID-19 pandemic when the country was in a state of despire, it was very evident that the core of every Ghanaian was to stay Alife amidst the pandemic. Everyone wanted to do everything possible to stay Alife. We leverage this mindset to enhance a very strong empathic relationship with the consumers and the general public to drive the brand name with the core objective of 'Being There' to keep the hope of every Ghanaian of being Alife

02

The Creative Idea

For the Alife soap brand, main point of focus was how it was going to integrate itself into the media scene and still stay relevant and communicate its effectiveness in the washing of hands to stay healthy and safe. Hence, we produced the idea "Stay Alive with Alife Soap" campaign. The Creative Idea was to connect and drive a very strong empathy with the mindset of most Ghanaians of just wanting to stay Alife amidst the uncertainties of COVID-19

03

The Strategy

Our strategy was predominantly driven by the habits that can give the consumer the reason to act in ways that will enhance their dire need to stay alive. At this point, there was not clear and strong awareness around the key protocols of hand washing as a key life safer during the pandemic. Our strategy was to leverage key TV moments and occasions to drive home the importance of hand washing to stay alive. Hence we created a core platform of Alife Soap Titbits riding on the big idea of 'Stay Alive with Alife Soap'.

04

The Execution

TV: we created a bigger than life experience for consumers to watch the brand impact in their lives by being there with tips on how to be alive with washing of hands and other COVID-19 protocols presented in a 'non scary' format.
RADIO:
Engaged On-air personalities (OAPs) to drive communications around how to keep safe and healthy during the COVID-19 The presenters talks about precautionary ways of keeping safe during the COVID-19 and integrating the core brand benefit of Alife soap into the engagement within their programming

05

Result

Within the first 5 weeks, there was over 21k cartons sold across markets in Ghana (This is unprecedented within the business). Campaign Reach was 79% be end of the period

Credits

Michael Jacquaye, mediaReachOMD, Manager

A-Life Soap Campaign

Background

The Brand, Alife Soap has never been on air. During the COVID-19 pandemic when the country was in a state of despire, it was very evident that the core of every Ghanaian was to stay Alife amidst the pandemic. Everyone wanted to do everything possible to stay Alife. We leverage this mindset to enhance a very strong empathic relationship with the consumers and the general public to drive the brand name with the core objective of 'Being There' to keep the hope of every Ghanaian of being Alife and give an aura of hope on key life saving tips during the pandemic tied to the core brand name and brand essence. The connection was strong, the impact was felt and the business result evident considering that it was the first time ever that the Alife soap brand was having an on-air media activation, hence needed to drive more engagement with our core target audience

Creative Idea

The challenging factor for the airing of the Alife Soap was based on the fact that there were the influx of many soap and sanitizing brands that suddenly churned out during the pandemic period, with all communication the killing of 99.9% germs and bacteria. For the Alife soap brand, main point of focus was how it was going to integrate itself into the media scene and still stay relevant and communicate its effectiveness in the washing of hands to stay healthy and safe. Hence we came up with the idea "Stay Alive with Alife Soap" campaign. The Creative Idea was to connect and drive a very strong empathy with the mindset of most Ghanaians of just wanting to stay Alife amidst the uncertainties of COVID-19

Strategy

Our strategy was predominantly driven by the habits that can give the consumer the reason to act in ways that will enhance their dire need to stay alive. At this point, there was not clear and strong awareness around the key protocols of hand washing as a key life safer during the pandemic. Our strategy was to leverage key TV moments and occasions to drive home the importance of hand washing to stay alive- Hence we created a core platform of Alife Soap Titbits riding on the big idea of 'Stay Alive with Alife Soap'

Execution

TV: Due to budget, the brand couldn't afford a TVC. However, we created a bigger than life experience for consumers to watch the brand impact in their lives by being there with tips on how to be alive with washing of hands and other COVID-19 protocols presented in a 'non scary' format.

We leveraged and creatively created segments on the Afternoon and Evening news, where we integrate contents that educates on how to stay safe within the pandemic period and why it is necessary to wash one's hands. The creatives takes over the help/bottom side of the TV during well viewed contents.

RADIO:

Engaged On-air personalities (OAPs) to drive communications around how to keep safe and healthy during the COVID-19 era. Stations across Accra and Kumasi markets were engaged for this campaign. The presenters talks about precautionary ways of keeping safe during the COVID-19 and integrating the core brand benefit of Alife soap into the engagement within their programming.

Results

Within the first 5 weeks, there was over 21k cartons sold across markets in Ghana (This is unprecedented within the business). Campaign Reach was 79% be end of the period.

BRAND   William Grant & Sons
ENTRANT COMPANY   Mediafuse Dentsu - Vizeum, Lagos, Nigeria
AWARD   Bronze

Glenfiddich - Where Next?

Credits

Radley Connor, William Grant & Sons, Senior Regional Marketing Manager

Lauren Kritzinger, William Grant & Sons, Head of Marketing MEA

Joshua Oyeleye, Vizeum, Media Manager

Olajumoke Ajayi, Vizeum, Media Exec

Korede Ladejobi, Posterscope, OOH Asst. Managet

Micheal Ogundimu, Prodigy, Media Services Works

Nosa Ojo, Prodigy, Managing Director

Akintude Akinola, iProspect, Digital Account Manager

Stephanie Ume, iProspect, Digital Account Exec

Glenfiddich - Where Next?

Background

Glenfiddich is the world's most awarded single malt whiskey and for 130 years the brand has constantly challenged the status quo & pushed the boundaries.

Glenfiddich recently launched into the Nigerian market but has grown to become the #1 selling single malt whisky with a strong on trade presence. Despite this growth, brand awareness is still relatively low compared to its key competitors.

Glenfiddich also needed to build emotional connection with consumers and elevate its luxury credentials through effective deployment of the brand's creative assets.

We were briefed to deliver an integrated media strategy and plan for Glenfiddich Nigeria and demonstrate how this will be applied across the various media channels. We were also required to provide a rationale for the media/channel choices.

Due to the low awareness and early brand life stage in the market, the Stag's Story was essential to drive distinctive brand assets value, and increase likelihood of higher mental availability.

Creative Idea

The Glenfiddich Where Next campaign was created with an aim to inspire consumers to step out of their comfort zone, encouraging them to embrace risk in order to grow by continually asking themselves, Where Next?

The campaign idea celebrates the growth that can come through continually taking risks.

To build meaning for the brand we identified a key distinctive brand asset, which was the logo/stag - as a key distinctive element that possesses a unique ability to become prominent enough to increase associative memory networks and further establish mental availability for Glenfiddich. Bringing this to life required that we enable a rich storytelling experience in our communications through innovative executions that truly embodies our Maverick Spirit.

In summary we sought to build on brand equity, with the goal of creating stature and meaning at scale and while establishing Glenfiddich as a motivating symbol of taking risks to grow.

Strategy

Our strategy was to create a brand message so distinctive and relevant that it attracts far beyond its current base. Our target audience are Mavericks of both genders. They consider themselves a work in progress – always striving for self-growth, learning new skills, and challenging their own views. Our Mavericks were categorized into three (3) broad groups.

The 90% target – Maverick Crowds are light buyers of the category but represent a broad consumption pool.

The 9% target – Irrepressible Mavericks are change makers who already have a strong affinity to our luxury values and position.

The 1% target – Maverick Influencers are a small group of people with a big reach and impact on the wider population. The approach was to engage deeply with our 1% & 9% to generate advocacy while spreading our message far as possible across the 90% via paid & earned media while actively seeking conversion.

Execution

As a luxury brand, we could not compromise media quality for reach/cost, hence we aimed for premium positioning, beautiful formats, and a flawless end to end experience across all touchpoints. Using Dentsu's proprietary tool CCS, we could see this audience is one that likes to continually learn new things, showing strong penetration across the lines of technology and innovation and strong indexes for News, Politics and Documentaries.

Our tools and insights led us to identifying broad reach channels that allow more emotional storytelling such as online video, advocacy, TV, social and OOH.

To penetrate the 90% Maverick Crowd, we deployed short form online video, audiovisual on TV and high impact Out of Home. For the 9% Irrepressible Mavericks we utilized standout Out of Home executions, online video, lifestyle magazines, content partnerships with influencers tagged the #GLENFIDDICHWHERENEXTLIVE series which featured real stories and inspirational memoirs from true Maverick spirits.

Results

Overall, the Glenfiddich Where Next campaign reached over 40M+ across TV, OOH and Digital.

The TV commercial was placed on high attention TV programming across status building channels with high scale such as National Geographic, CNN, ESPN etc. and we achieved 921 GRPs across Open and Pay TV.

Aside from client feedback pertaining to the standout execution and cost savings achieved through extensive negotiations, the special builds OOH executions were recognized and applauded by consumers on social media as an impactful way to stand out from the regular OOH formats. Social and mobile ads placed in socially native ways and speaking to different social media consumption behaviours resulted in top results such as the cost per instream view of $0.0087, which is a very positive result compared to the industry benchmark of $0.02.

A study conducted by Facebook post-campaign shows a strong brand lift was recorded during the period of the campaign when compared to brands in same vertical. Standard ad recall and ad favorability amongst the test group was +22.1% and +31.1% respectively.

BRAND International Breweries
ENTRANT COMPANY Mediafuse Dentsu - Vizeum, Lagos, Nigeria
AWARD Silver

Budweiser Kings Of Football Tv Show

Budweiser Kings Of Football Tv Show

Credits

Joshua Oyeleye, Vizeum Media, Manager

Olajumoke Okikiolu, IB PLC, Marketing Manager

Tolulope Adedeji, IB PLC, Marketing Director

Dubem Orji, IB PLC, Brand Manager

Olajumoke Ajayi, Vizeum Media, Planning Exec

Samuel Adeniyi, Vizeum Media, Buying

Akinola Akintunde, iProspect, Digital Account Manager

Kehinde Allen, Isobar, Art Director

Chinonso Wilson, Isobar, Account Exec

Nana Fischer, Isobar, Account Manager

Halima Bakenne, Isobar, Content Manager

Budweiser Kings Of Football Tv Show

Background

The Budweiser Kings of Football show was created to elevate the position of the brand as official sponsors of the English Premier League and La Liga and grow SOV on Supersport (#1 Football Entertainment platform in Africa).

We were set to launch the second phase of the 2020/21 football season campaign in January 2021, however learnings from the past executions showed that we had some challenge with cut through and engagement. It was clear we had to improve the entertainment factor and appeal of the show.

To optimize the show, we decided to test four (4) different TV show concepts. Following the test, we discovered that consumers were showing a higher preference for shows where they can have a voice. Fan involvement stood as a very important factor, consumers wanted an environment of socializing and friendly rivalry.

By engaging the right influencer and gamifying the situation, we created a social strategy that helped to re-energize football fans all over Nigeria.

Creative Idea

Introducing the new Kings of Football Game Show, the ultimate lifestyle and football trivia game show!

The new Kings of football show was created to bring football fans closer to the greatness on and off the pitch to inspire them to seize their opportunity and celebrate their time to shine.

Three (3) hosts and six (6) consumers will grace the stage every week till the end of the 2020/21 football season. The six (6) contestants will form two (2) teams who will compete against each other for a 1Million naira prize to be given away on every episode. The contestants will be tested on their knowledge about everything Football from the English premier league to the Spanish La Liga.

The game show was structured into two halves like a typical soccer match, with categories such as Kick Off, Through Pass, VAR, Penalty etc. During the half time we create engagement using Fantasy Premier League, Fans Zone Vox Pop and Skype Call sessions with celebs and pundits.

Strategy

Our strategy was to create a TV show so distinctive and relevant that it attracts far beyond its current base. And we intended to achieve this by establishing ourselves as a brand that brings fans closer to the greatness on and off the pitch inspiring them to seize opportunity and celebrate their time to shine.

For the first phase of the relaunch show we focused on embedding a cultural layer, aiming to win the hearts of more football fans between the ages of 18-44. Major brand ambassadors were selected to tease the announcement of the new Brand Ambassador, leveraging their potential appeal to a broader audience.

For the second phase, the brand announced Ozo as a new Brand Ambassador with comms on Radio and Social Media.

The third phase had Ozo make his first appearance as co-host on the KOF show which premiered on the 28th of February 2021.

Execution

Hardly any other medium reaches the football loving beer drinkers as accurately as Super Sport, Africa's first 24/7 Sports broadcaster. So together with Super Sport, we developed and co-produced the Kings of Football Show, a one-hour TV game show recorded every Thursday and premiered on Sundays. The show is hosted by two male hosts (Jimmie and Ozo) and a female host (Ose) who are always in the company of the resident DJ Dips always keeping the energy levels up and up.

Over eight (8) Sundays, Budweiser has presented the most engaging football gameshow ever seen on TV. From opening graphics, verbal mentions, quality of questions, set design and custom vox pop content, Budweiser dominated this premium, one-hour time block as well as various other repeat slots on across Super Sport channels every week.

Consumers who want to participate are encouraged to register on www.budweiserngeria.com.ng/kofshow and each participating team stands a chance to win up to 1Million naira on every episode.

Results

Budweiser Kings of Football Show was the #1 TV show on Super Sport primetime besides live football matches, with an average rating of 4.7 (MF, ABC, 18-44) recording a viewership growth of (+16% YOY) within the first month of evaluation.

Social media was also full of praise as Ozo's reveal as the brand's new BA and co-host of the KOF show generated over 14,000 tweets with over 96% positive sentiment and 82.5% predominant emotion on joy.

On the 28th of February 2021, when the new edition of the Budweiser Kings of Football show went live with the brand's newest ambassador, Ozo, as new co-host. The results were phenomenal in numbers and conversation on social media, especially Twitter. Budweiser created such huge positive PR buzz across social media with both hashtags #BudFootball & #KingsofFootballShow becoming #1 twitter trending topic in Nigeria.

The KOF Show crew have visited 4 (four) bars in eight (8) weeks and interviewed over 30 fans on the KOF Fans Zone Vox Pop segment. The entire Football campaign has aided Budweiser to reach 18.2MM+ people within the campaign period.

BRAND   Safaricom PLC
ENTRANT COMPANY   Dentsu Aegis Network Kenya, Nairobi, Kenya
AWARD   Gold

The Bantering Billboard

Credits

Gideon Ruita, Dentsu Aegis Network-Kenya, Account Director

Alex Tutu, Dentsu Aegis Network-Kenya, Managing Director

Teresa Makori, Dentsu Aegis Network-Kenya, Associate Creative Director

Stuti Ahuja, Safaricom PLC, Brand Manager

Stella Arithi, Safaricom PLC, Brand Manager

Amelia Aganda, Safaricom PLC, Brand Manager

Miriam Waititu, Dentsu Aegis Network-Kenya, Business Unit Head

The Bantering Billboard

Background
Safaricom, the biggest telecommunications company in Kenya, was celebrating their 20-year anniversary and they wanted to make it about making it about their consumers and engaging with their consumers. Their message to Kenyans was two simple words: "Twende Tukiuke", meaning, "Let's go beyond."
So, we set out to bring the message home to each one of them, with a first of its kind out of home execution.

Creative Idea
To mark 20 years of serving Kenyans, Safaricom, Kenya's biggest telecommunications company had one unifying message with two simple words, "Twende Tukiuke", meaning, "Let's go beyond."
To truly live this, they wanted to go above and beyond by including Kenyans in their celebrations in a very personal way.
We used this opportunity to install a campaign that would utilise the flexibility of DOOH with the dwell time and we came up with a digital billboard that would not only interact and draw the attention of our audience.

Strategy
First using Google Mobility reports, we were able to identify Nairobi's busiest round about that would offer us the ample dwell time to run our execution. We then used KURA (Kenya Urban Roads Authority) data to identify the peak traffic hours where we could engage with motorists stuck in traffic.

Execution
We installed a camera on the digital screen at the University Way round about facing inbound traffic. The Camera, using AI and machine learning was able to identify the make colour and model of the vehicles and customise a shout out to the motorists based on the above metrics projected on the screen. The message on the screen also broke down what "Kiuke" meant to Kenyan commuters and in the end asked them to hoot twice or give a response to engage with us.

Results
Over the course of 8 weeks, we were able to serve over 28000 unique messages and were able to reach a peak of 58k Impressions daily from the interaction with the screen thereby truly harnessing the power of an offline platform in delivering online traction, talk-ability and measurable results.

MEET THE DIGITAL / GOOD JURORS

PRESIDENT
JULIET EHIMUAN
Director, Google Nigeria

EMMANUEL AMAKWAH
Creative Director
Now Available Africa, Accra, Ghana

SOLOMON OSAFILE
Creative Lead
The RedWolf Company, Lagos, Nigeria

ALEMU EMURON
Chief Creative Officer
Betika.com, Nairobi, Kenya

OBINNA CHUKU
Partner & Creative Director
Bloom Interactive, Accra, Ghana

MARIAM AYOADE
Director Media/Digital
VISA, Sub Saharan Africa

KARIM YERMECHE
Chief Executive Officer
Lotus Conseil, Hydra, Algeria

Apps, Messaging, Social Media Campaign, Website, Covid, For Profit, Non Profit

App

BRAND   Canbebe

ENTRANT COMPANY   SHIFTIN, Algiers, Algeria

AWARD   Bronze

Canbebe Mobile App

Credits

Majda Nafissa Rahal, SHIFTIN, Associate Director

Chouaib Attoui, SHIFTIN, Associate Director

Roufaida Djouad,i SHIFTIN, Project Manager

Houssem Teghri, SHIFTIN, UI/UX Designer

Canbebe Mobile App

Creative Idea

In a very crowded Algerian diapers market, innovation is what allows a brand to stand out. Parents are more connected than ever and constantly looking for the right resources online to help them with their babies.

We worked with the baby products brand Canbebe to offer the Algerian parents a creative digital tool to take care of their little ones. We set out to create the ultimate mobile app for parents, and thought out the functionalities to be very useful, with a playful and easy-to-use interface.

The app features a digital healthbook to track the baby's vaccination and health metrics. It also allows you to find the nearest pediatrician thanks to a geo-located MD directory. It also offers a curated list of helpful articles. All the while highlighting the brands' products, events and promotions.

This app is the first of its kind in Algeria, and for the whole Ontex Group globally. It offers a unique brand experience that is soon to be extended to other North-African countries.

Execution

From design to development, everything was tailor-made for Canbebe.

In designing the app, we kept our target audience in mind while bringing out the brand's style. Young moms and parents want something that is playful, intuitive and fun to use. Making the user experience super easy but also attractive and visually pleasing was our goal.

For mobile development, we followed a hybrid approach with an agile methodology. We made sure that the app remained pixel-perfect when handover from design to development. Then we sparkled in delightful animations to keep users engaged throughout their journey on the app.

The whole process took a little over three months. In a short period, we could create a new brand touch point that is at the heart of the brand strategy and customer acquisition.

The app launch campaign included influencer marketing, ad buy on social media (Facebook and Instagram) and could gather close to 10k downloads in less than 2 weeks.

Credits

Ilyas Lahmer, SHIFTIN, Back-end Developer

Abdenour Nacer Bey, SHIFTIN, Fron-end Developer

Chakib Diboun, Canbebe, Digital Manager Maghreb

Mustapha Saari, Canbebe, Marketing Manager Maghreb

Messaging

BRAND	Guiness
ENTRANT COMPANY	digitXplus, Lagos, Nigeria
AWARD	Shortlist

Guinness - Your First Drink On Us

Credits

Timilehin Oyedeji, digitXplus, Account Lead

Guinness - Your First Drink On Us

Background
Due to the impact of COVID-19 pandemic in 2020, Nigeria went into lockdown in March 2020. As a result of the lockdown, non-essential businesses/services (including bars) were shut down in adherence to the social distancing measures put in place by the government.

The lockdown was lifted in August 2020 and bars started re-opening sometimes in September, however strict Social Distancing norms continued, Guinness Nigeria needed to launch the new beer product – Guinness Smooth but couldn't do so much considering social distancing and gathering restrictions as placed by the Government.

The challenge was to find a way to drive trials of the new Guinness smooth.

Creative Idea
Consumers were eagerly waiting to visit their favorite bars because that's the place they like to hangout with friends over a game while enjoying beer

Guinness Nigeria looked at this as a big opportunity and wanted to welcome 200,000 consumers back into the bars with a free bottle of Guinness Smooth to induce trails

Bars were officially opened towards the end of September, hence we planned to tactically leverage on the Nigerian Independence Day on October 1, by tying this "independence" from the movement restrictions to the Independence as a country and communicate the message: "Independence, Your First Drink On Us".

Also, to celebrate not just the "re-opening" of the bars, but Nigeria as a great country, the feeling of going out to get hang with friends at that "cool" spot but also to celebrate the Launch of Guinness Smooth

Strategy
Seeing that there was a huge surge on digital due to the pandemic, and our target audience were always on these platforms, we thought to leverage on mobile and technology solution to connect with our target audience and get them to take the desired action, with little or no human contact as they grab their Free Guinness Smooth Bottle, at a bar closest to them

Execution
We leveraged on artificial intelligence on WhatsApp to engage our target audience and walk them through the journey of getting them a unique code for redemption at a bar closest to them. With the WhatsApp AI BOT, we were able to perform age gating, ask our audience where they stay/live; then advise them of a bar closest to them.

We also leverage on the USSD code "1759" to also cater to some of our target audience in remote areas who might have just a feature phone or might not have data.

Results
At the end of the campaign, a total of 96,684 vouchers were generated through the WhatsApp BOT and USSD code, out of which 64,788 vouchers were redeemed at the various bars across the country.

Social Media **Campaigns**

BRAND	MALTINA
ENTRANT COMPANY	Noah's Ark Communications Limited, Lagos, Nigeria
AWARD	Shortlist

Maltina Variants

Credits

Lanre Adisa, Noah's Ark Communications Limited, Chief creative Officer

Bolaji Alausa, Noah's Ark Communications Limited, Executive Creative Director

Maurice Ugwonoh, Noah's Ark Communications Limited, Creative Director

Solomon Osafile, Noah's Ark Communications Limited, Deputy Creative Director

Adedeji Adeleke, Noah's Ark Communications Limited, Planner

Ife Tabi, Noah's Ark Communications Limited, Planner

Gabriel Olonisakin, Noah's Ark Communications Limited, Art Director

Kazeem Lawal, Noah's Ark Communications Limited, Art Director

Toke Mabayomije, Noah's Ark Communications Limited, Copywriter

Segun Odejimi, Noah's Ark Communications Limited, Copywriter

Jumoke Akinyele, Noah's Ark Communications Limited, Brand Manager

Maltina Variants

Background
The largest Malt market in Africa and 3rd in the world? That is Nigeria. The Malt brand than had historically led the park? That "was" Maltina. But like most head honchos, threats abound. As such, leading up to 2019 since 2016, the brand had seen a year-on-year decline in market share, and while recovered, was stagnating. As such, we needed to unlock growth. Over indexing among 25 to 34-year-olds who were a relatively small segment of the population, while competing malt brands to whom Maltina was losing market share at the time, had more penetration levels among 18 to 24-year-olds. Something was wrong. However, that was less than half of the story. You see, in Nigeria like most African countries, 18 to 24-year-olds (Life Maximizers) form a significant part of the population.

Brand Objective
Create a youthful affinity for the brand
Dial-up excitement within the category
Grow salience for the brand in the youth segment

Creative Idea
Own The Flavour
This was an idea that suggested the variety of experiences that was out there for the "young explorers" to enjoy, while functionally placing the new flavors of Maltina as the center of consumption occasions for the TG.

Strategy
With our target audience surgically defined, young Nigerians (18 -24-year-old) who were on the cusp of adulthood and independence. Wary of the responsibilities and pressures that come with adulthood, but poised not to lose the joy of experiencing all there was to explore. We called them - "Young Explorers". The plan was to put Maltina, a brand that was previously not on their wavelength, at the center of their exploration (across multiple consumption occasions). In doing this, however, we created new variants (Pineapple and Vanilla flavors) to appeal to the explorative tendencies of the "young explorers"

Execution
Leading with an impactful OOH and Digital Strategy, we leveraged the power of influencer marketing to drive engagement with this new crop of consumers – the Life Maximizers … the Flavour Geng …To Achieve Broad Reach: we deployed OOH (LEDs, Lampoles & Massive Billboards) & engaging Radio Communication (ROS, Hypes & In-Store Radio) to quickly drive mental availability with the volume target. To Achieve Targeted Reach: we dialed up engagement on Digital & Mobile with engaging content from our influencers and UGC from consumers. We supported with TV and PR Amplification to drive Top of Mind and sustenance of the campaign.

Results
Volumes: We delivered +118khl in less than 4 months… (+36% above target) … Delivering a sales uplift of 30% on the total brand….
Consumers Reached: We engaged and sampled over 700,000 consumers across channels
Activations: we executed +100 activations (in Key Accounts, Modern Trade, In Market, Consumer Events, etc)
MEDIA:
OOH: Deployed +518 OOH executions on – LED, Lampoles & Static Billboards
Radio: Deployed 5,069 Spots on Radio with an audience reach of +33.28m through – ROS, Hypes, In-Store Radio engagement, and sponsored programs.
TV: Deployed +620 Spots on Cable, Sponsored programs, In-Cinema Ad Spots, Squeeze backs & on CNN
Digital: Deployed engaging posts, videos, and User Generated Content across FB, IG, Twitter & YouTube …. Delivering +57m Impressions, 16m Unique Reach, 1.4m Engagement (with +17k Reactions) across all platforms combined.
PR Amplification: Reached +58.4m (Paid – 25.3m + Earned – 33.1m) through Print, Blog Posts, UGC from micro-influencers on Some.

Credits

Ojumitunrayo Olufade, Noah's Ark Communications Limited, Brand Manager

Olusukanmi Adebayo, Underdog Production, Head of Production

Funsho Adebayo, Underdog Production, Producer

Idowu Mattew, Underdog Production, Producer

Uche Nwaohiri, Underdog Production, Production Art Director

Patience Ugbe, Noah's Ark Communications Limited, Operations

Daniel Akintobi, Noah's Ark Communications Limited, Operations

BRAND	One Bank by Sterling
ENTRANT COMPANY	Webcoupers, Yaba, Lagos, Nigeria
AWARD	Shortlist

One Bank by Sterling

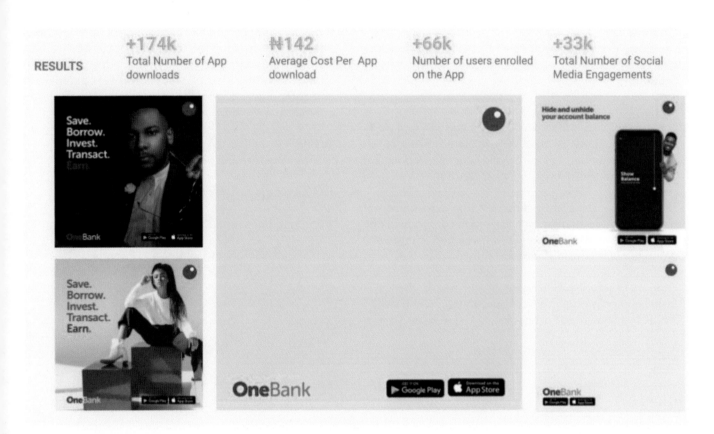

RESULTS

+174k
Total Number of App downloads

₦142
Average Cost Per App download

+66k
Number of users enrolled on the App

+33k
Total Number of Social Media Engagements

Credits

Peter Ajegbomogun, Webcoupers, Chief Digital Officer

Olumaiye Aladeniji, Webcoupers, Head of Creatives

Wole Fanegan, Webcoupers, Lead UI & UX design

Eyitayo Ajayi, Webcoupers, Lead New business

One Bank by Sterling

Background
Sterling Bank launched its flagship digital banking application to compete in a saturated financial products saturated ecosystem. The digital product is"OneBank by Sterling" and the MVP features are the ability to save, borrow, invest, transfer [globally] and earn.

Creative Idea
Develop a performance digital marketing framework that allow App download and App usage for One Banks by Sterling.

Strategy
The campaign Big Idea was built around the tagline "A New Way to Live/ A New Way to Bank" because we wanted to promote it as an holistic banking product that redefines financial fullment in one digital bank.

The big idea manifested in different forms across different phases of the campaign. First we laid the groundwork by building a landing page [view here] and community management on Instagram and Twitter.

Then we proceeded with two set of paid media; the first is Install campaigns [Universal App Campaign by Google, Twitter Install Ads and Facebook lead Gen Ads] and Social

Media Awareness Ads for the entire duration. While that was running we deployed a growth hacking strategy using Incentives on popular channels and influencers to get maximum reach within the desired Target Audience.

Execution
The use of digital marketing platform use as Google DV360, Facebook and Google Universal App Campaign were the primary channels for awareness and conversion. However, the campaign kicked off using the Creative A/B testing model to understand the best preferred creative for the campaign, during the campaign interest based optimization was done to improve the conversation

Results
+174k Total Number of App downloads

142 Average Cost Per App download

+66k Number of users enrolled on the App

+33k Total Number of Social Media Engagements.

BRAND   AIRTEL NIGERIA
ENTRANT COMPANY   Noah's Ark Communications Limited, Lagos, Nigeria
AWARD   Shortlist

Airtel TV (Amaka Must Go)

Credits

Lanre Adisa, Noah's Ark Communications Limited, Chief creative Officer

Bolaji Alausa, Noah's Ark Communications Limited, Executive Creative Director

Maurice Ugwonoh, Noah's Ark Communications Limited, Creative Director

Solomon Osafile, Noah's Ark Communications Limited, Deputy Creative Director

Adedeji Adeleke, Noah's Ark Communications Limited, Planner

Ezekiel Resedenz, Noah's Ark Communications Limited, Art Director

Maya Adeyemo, Noah's Ark Communications Limited, Art Director

Airtel TV (Amaka Must Go)

Background
Airtel TV is a free mobile first video-on-demand platform from one of Nigeria's powerhouse telco brands - Airtel
The platform, which is exclusive to Airtel simmers only, has a wide range of local and international content (movies, series, music videos, Live TV etc) available to consumers on a freemium and premium subscription basis. But that's just half of what Airtel TV really turned out to be.
This is an exposition of how we cheered up a nation during her lowest moment of 2020 with the power of content

Creative Idea
AMAKA MUST GO
And so, to lift the spirits of a nation with something close to what they've always wanted, we created the iconic "AMAKA MUST GO" trailer - a satiric story that gave a never before seen peep into the lives of the much loved Airtel characters.

Strategy
The democratized nature of the internet brings both legal and illegal platforms for content consumption at the disposal of consumers, how could we possibly introduce the Airtel TV platform whose KSPs (freemium subscription, mobile first, local & international content) were already available either independently or combined on some other platforms

Execution
With the use of a movie trailer trope, we produced a 2 minute movie trailer with the popular casts from "The In-Laws" (Airtel) in it.

Results
The IG Live fall-out drove massive speculation which made #AmakaMustGo and Airtel to be on the Twitter top 10 trend list for 2 days with top blogs like Instablog and Tundeednut organically picking up on the fall-out. The Amaka must go TVC garnered 1.8m views on Youtube, 7.1m views on Facebook, and 1.3m views on Twitter.

Online sentiment analysis of the comments and interactions showed 88% positive interactions all across the posts and videos.

While soft metrics such as video views, impressions, and likes flatter the campaign. The most rewarding for us was the attainment of Over 1 Million Plus Mobile Downloads in the first 6 months of the campaign.

Credits

Adetola Shode, Noah's Ark Communications Limited, Art Director

Jesujoba Popoola, Noah's Ark Communications Limited, Copywriter

Mayokun Ajayeoba, Noah's Ark Communications Limited, Copywriter

Judith Ezeali, Noah's Ark Communications Limited, Brand Manager

Abimbola Sanusi, Noah's Ark Communications Limited, Brand Manager

Patience Ugbe, Noah's Ark Communications Limited, Operations

Daniel Akintobi, Noah's Ark Communications Limited, Operations

Ife Tabi, Noah's Ark Communications Limited, Planner

BRAND   Budweiser
ENTRANT COMPANY   Isobar Nigeria, Lagos, Nigeria
AWARD   Shortlist

King is born

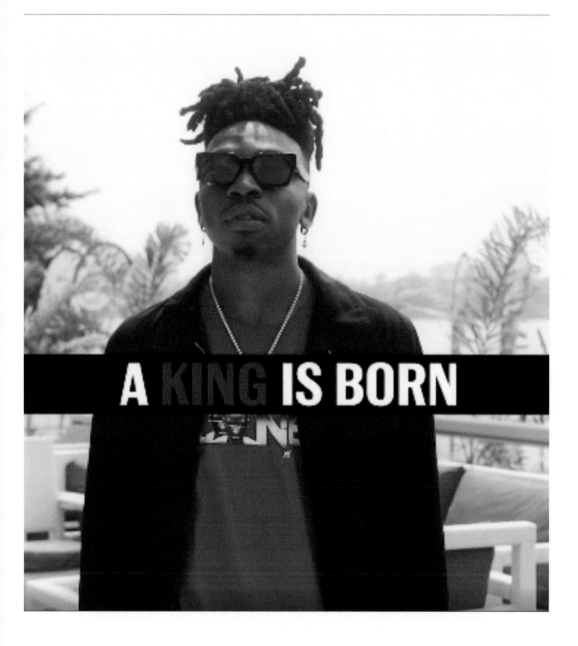

Credits

Abena Annan, Isobar, Client service

King is born

Background
Coming into 2020, we signed 2 new ambassadors for Budweiser and leveraged BUDxMiami to create a unique unveil campaign. For this campaign, we Leveraged the power of storytelling, social media, influencer and video marketing to create suspense, hype and leave consumers guessing who the new brand ambassadors are. Afterwards, we had an exclusive, invite only, event with fans where we had the official unveil of the ambassadors. After the unveil, our consumers followed the 2 new ambassadors to BUDxMiami where they got a unique experience of the event through the lenses of the brand ambassadors

Creative Idea
Social media has forever changed the way we create, place and consume content. However, one thing has remained the same throughout the years – people trust people more than they trust brands.

With that in mind, Budweiser identified two brand ambassadors who will act as representatives for the brand across multiple platforms. The task was to use the power of social media to announce to the world Budweiser's new brand ambassadors in a way that increases the brand's SOV

Strategy
While influencer influencer marketing has remained the number one marketing strategy for many brands, this heavy investment often yield unfruitful results. So, with Budweiser signing two new ambassadors, there was a new challenge.

How could we use social media to announce to the world Budweiser's new brand ambassadors in a way that increases the brand's SOV, build brand equity and generate earned media.

Execution
Leveraging the power of storytelling, social media, influencer and video marketing we themed our campaign – A King Is Born.

Our story created suspense and hype and left consumers guessing who the new brand ambassadors are. 24 hours before the unveil, we teased our consumers on social media with snippets of the unveil videos asking them to guess who the new brand ambassadors are for a chance to party with them at the unveil party.

We syndicated this piece of content to our existing brand influencers who helped drive the conversation. The day we unveiled; Budweiser dominated the conversation on Twitter for two consecutive days as consumers changed their profile names to #KingBudweiser, #BudweiserXMike, #AKingIsBorn among many others.

The brand also organically trended for 2 days with the following hashtags: #AKingIsBorn, and KingMikeXBudweiser

Results
70,980.27 in Earned Media Value,
6.300,000+ Impressions,
332,000+ Engagements
930,000+ video views
10% growth in Social Followership

BRAND   AIRTEL NIGERIA
ENTRANT COMPANY Noah's Ark Communications Limited, Lagos, Nigeria
AWARD   Shortlist

444

Credits

Lanre Adisa, Noah's Ark Communications Limited, Chief creative Officer

Bolaji Alausa, Noah's Ark Communications Limited, Executive Creative Director

Maurice Ugwonoh, Noah's Ark Communications Limited, Creative Director

Solomon Osafile, Noah's Ark Communications Limited, Deputy Creative Director

Adedeji Adeleke, Noah's Ark Communications Limited, Planner

Ezekiel Resedenz, Noah's Ark Communications Limited, Art Director

Maya Adeyemo, Noah's Ark Communications Limited, Art Director

Background

Over the years, Mobile Network services have grown inextricably intertwined with financial services. Although the financial service providers (banks) have always been the ones reaping the benefits of transaction costs with their digital banking solutions such as short codes that enable transactions (buying airtime, data etc) directly from customers' bank accounts. Also, with customer often having multiple bank accounts and consequently, needing multiple short codes, Airtel came up with her own short code, which can singularly help her customers recharge directly from all their bank accounts - *444#

Creative Idea

"444 is a Meta4" for easy mobile transactions.

From the single minded thought, the creative idea naturally leaned towards having fun with the code in itself - 444 being 4 in three places was translated to Meta4 (which when said sounded like a pop-culture-ish/Yoruba way of calling out the code). With the idea settled, it was time for the art itself - a jingle that would make its way to the very top of the Nigerian music scene. The jingle had to appeal to the "streets", yet appealing to the elites (similar to the naira-marley effect). To cut the long story short, we nailed it and it was an instant hit

Strategy

Communication Objective

Get the 444 short code to achieved a household level recall among Airtel and non-Airtel users

Business Objective

Increase short code usage by 200% in first 4 weeks of campaign launch

Strategic Approach

With our objectives, two things were clear
We needed high levels of recall. We needed high level of salience (that is people needed to strongly associate *444# with the key service attributes - easy recharge and convenience. Essentially making it a "metaphor" for convenient and easy recharge from bank accounts. Hence our single minded thought; 444 is a metaphor for easy mobile transactions.

Execution

The campaign which was initially designed to be powered by a jingled, ended up being heavily driven by video by popular demand. We created a video for the jingle and ran it in digital channels.

Results

From a business point of view, we totally smashed the targets, where we were required to increase the short code usage by 200% in the first 4 weeks of the campaign, we achieved over 900% increase in first 4 weeks (these are 7 digits figures for context). The campaign garnered hit reviews and views on various digital platforms. - and reached over 11 million people across Facebook, Twitter, Instagram, and Youtube. As well as over 500,000 engagement instances (likes, comments, retweets, and shares)

The campaign further garnered even more engagement during the Big Brother Naija show, where housemates were required to do their covers - a period where Airtel and 444 were the most talked about subjects in social media

Credits

Adetola Shode, Noah's Ark Communications Limited, Art Director

Jesujoba Popoola, Noah's Ark Communications Limited, Copywriter

Mayokun Ajayeoba, Noah's Ark Communications Limited, Copywriter

Judith Ezeali, Noah's Ark Communications Limited, Brand Manager

Abimbola Sanusi, Noah's Ark Communications Limited, Brand Manager

Patience Ugbe, Noah's Ark Communications Limited, Operations

Daniel Akintobi, Noah's Ark Communications Limited, Operations

Ife Tabi, Noah's Ark Communications Limited, Planner

BRAND Airtel Nigeria

ENTRANT COMPANY Noah's Ark Communications Limited, Lagos, Nigeria

AWARD Shortlist

Airtel Mobile Number Portability *(Tailor)*

AIRTEL
Smart Talk

Challenge:
Create a campaign that will get existing "high-value" competition customers to switch to Airtel and make it their primary network.

The Objective:
From our research and client's data, we knew that in spite of the loose nature of the category - where people had multiple sims, category consumers usually had a primary sim that housed the highest chunk of their monthly spend. We knew if we could make Airtel that sim, we could win.

Therefore, our objective took a more tangible shape - Get high-value competition customers to make Airtel their primary network.

The creative idea:
Change Your Tailor, Keep Your Swag
This is based on the insight we got after a survey that showed people always want the best especially when they can afford it, and they don't mind switching to a different source just to keep it the best.

Execution
We brought it closer to home, leveraging the experiences of the target audience by asking - what were those things that people sometimes hold on to for sentimental reason in spite of the dissapointments. Among many examples, "The Tailor" was reverberating. The averge Nigerian's experience usually included that one tailor who was so good, but unrealiable.

The campaign was video led, and utilized social media, and television as the main channels

Result:
The campaign video garnered hit reviews and views on various digital platforms. - with over 8.6 million views accross Facebook, Twitter, Instagram and Youtube. As well as over 76,000 enagement instances (likes, comments, retweets and shares) Online sentiment analysis of the comments and interactions showed a 82% positive interactions all across the posts and videos.

Credits

Lanre Adisa, Noah's Ark Communications Limited, Chief creative Officer

Bolaji Alausa, Noah's Ark Communications Limited, Executive Creative Director

Maurice Ugwonoh, Noah's Ark Communications Limited, Creative Director

Solomon Osafile, Noah's Ark Communications Limited, Deputy Creative Director

Adedeji Adeleke, Noah's Ark Communications Limited, Planner

Ezekiel Resedenz, Noah's Ark Communications Limited, Art Director

Adetola Shode, Noah's Ark Communications Limited, Art Director

Maya Adeyemo, Noah's Ark Communications Limited, Art Director

Jesujoba Popoola, Noah's Ark Communications Limited, Copywriter

Airtel Mobile Number Portability *(Tailor)*

Background

The Nigerian Mobile Network category has always been one that is quite loose, with customers usually hovering among networks; sometimes having up to 4 sims/network providers at once. Although campaigns and promotional offers, often momentarily dictate which network some customers use per time. This wasn't sustainable for the long term growth that Airtel yearned. In spite of the loose nature of the category, Airtel wanted a switch to her network to be a bit more permanent, so as to generate long term growth. The "million-dollar" question was how?

Creative Idea

Creative Idea: Change Your Tailor, Keep Your Swag. Our creative idea gleaned strongly from the strategy and the consumer research. We brought it closer to home, leveraging the experiences of the target audience by asking - what were those things that people sometimes hold on to for sentimental reasons in spite of the disappointments. Among many examples, "The Tailor " was reverberating, The average Nigerian's experience usually included that one tailor who was so good, but unreliable. And in Airtel fashion, we have a campaign idea - Change Your Tailor, Keep Your Swag - that mirrors the strategy.

Strategy

From our research and client's data, we knew that in spite of the loose nature of the category - where people had multiple sims, category consumers usually had a primary sim that housed the highest chunk of their monthly spend. We knew if we could make Airtel that sim, we could win. After a series of Focused Group Discussions (FGDs) and surveys, we realized the following

1. Consumers are always open to switching but will rather get a secondary sim.
2. They keep their primary number because it is of sentimental value (usually the first sim they ever had)
3. Even when service may not be the best on their primary sim, the fear of what to expect if they port is what keeps them. With all these insights, we knew consumers saw all MNOs as the same, so blowing our trumpets may not be the way to go, rather used this insight to play up the consequence of not porting and benefits of porting to nudge conversion.

Execution

We brought it closer home, leveraging the experiences of the target audience by asking - what were those things that people sometimes hold on to for sentimental reasons in spite of disappointments. Among many examples "The Tailor" was reverberating, The average Nigerian's experience usually included that one tailor who was so good, but unreliable. The campaign was video led, and utilized social media, and television as the main channels

Results

The campaign video garnered hit reviews and views on various digital platforms. - with over 8.6 million views across Facebook, Twitter, Instagram and YouTube. As well as over 76,000 engagement instances (likes, comments, retweets and shares). Online sentiment analysis of the comments and interactions showed 82% positive interactions all across the posts and videos.

On the business side, the number of ported numbers is growing considerably higher than before, with a record breaking projection by the end of the fiscal year.

Credits

Mayokun Ajayeoba, Noah's Ark Communications Limited, Copywriter

Judith Ezeali, Noah's Ark Communications Limited, Brand Manager

Abimbola Sanusi, Noah's Ark Communications Limited, Brand Manager

Patience Ugbe, Noah's Ark Communications Limited, Operations

BRAND   Beiersdorf
ENTRANT COMPANY   Isobar, Lagos, Nigeria
AWARD   Campaign Shortlist

Nivea Dry

Café

Credits

Abena Annan, Isobar Nigeria, Senior Group head, Client service

Nivea Dry

Background
The brand's Deo range didn't have a strong presence on digital so the plan was to strengthen its positioning through a digital-focused campaign.

Creative Idea
With #ClearTheAir, the idea was to employ humour in creating awareness to our target audience on the need to get rid of unpleasant body odour because it turns people off.

Strategy
The #ClearTheAir campaign was birthed to address the sensitive topic of body odour to the TA. To deliver precision targeting our primary target audience were males and females ages 18-40 who have active lifestyles and are always on the move. They also put a lot into looking and feeling good, but the humid weather can make them sweaty and stinky.

Execution
The campaign kicked off with the announcement of the brand's partnership with popular Nigerian artiste, Skiibii and multi-talented actress, Beverly Naya.

The campaign ran for 4 months and drove conversations around body odour across different touchpoints. We partnered with 3rd party media platforms to engage their audience and hit the streets to educate consumers about body odour, this was amplified online and generated a lot of buzz.

We also launched an online video series featuring two of the hottest Instagram Comedy influencers to highlight different relatable scenarios where you can encounter someone with body odour. In less than a month, we had hit 1.8m organic reach on one of the videos.

Throughout the duration of the campaign, we were able to keep the NIVEA Dry products as top of mind when it comes to tackling body odour while encouraging our TA to smell nice by using the NIVEA range of dry deodorants.

Results
The campaign kicked off with the announcement of the brand's partnership with popular Nigerian artiste, Skiibii and multi-talented actress, Beverly Naya.

The campaign ran for 4 months and drove conversations around body odour across different touchpoints. We partnered with 3rd party media platforms to engage their audience and hit the streets to educate consumers about body odour, this was amplified online and generated a lot of buzz.

We also launched an online video series featuring two of the hottest Instagram Comedy influencers to highlight different relatable scenarios where you can encounter someone with body odour. In less than a month, we had hit 1.8m organic reach on one of the videos.

Throughout the duration of the campaign, we were able to keep the NIVEA Dry products as top of mind when it comes to tackling body odour while encouraging our TA to smell nice by using the NIVEA range of dry deodorants.

Nivea Dry

Gym

Nivea Dry

Taxi

BRAND   TBWA/Concept
ENTRANT COMPANY   TBWA/Concept, Lagos, Nigeria
AWARD   Bronze

End Sars Campaign

End Sars Campaign

Background
Special Anti Robbery Squad (SARS) is a rogue unit of the Nigeria Police Force with a track record of abusing and harassing young Nigerians. They do this through unlawful marginalization and indiscriminate profiling of the people. Their alleged crimes include extortion, harassment, unlawful arrest, brutality, and even killing.
Fed up with these abuses and the government's failed promises, the youths took to the streets in October 2020 to protest and call for the disbandment of this notorious unit.

Creative Idea
Just like the slogan for the campaign 'Soro Soke', the creative idea is a clarion call to brands to speak up against police brutality.

Strategy
While the youths risked it all to make their voices heard, there was something else that was very loud- the silence of corporate Nigeria.

How do we call out brands without calling them out? We speak their language.

Execution
Brands have a voice- it's in their color, tone of voice, taglines etc. the idea is to speak to them in the language they will understand- their own.

Results
The campaign generated over 100,000 impressions and 500,000 reach in one week. this includes likes, comments and shares.

Credits

Wayne Samuel, TBWA/Concept, Copywriter

Kel Nwuke, TBWA/Concept, Art Director

Chinwe Onuoha, TBWA/Concept, Copy Manager

Biose Isichie, TBWA/Concept, Digital Strategist

Yusuf Adejumo, TBWA/Concept, Dep. Creative Director

Oyinda Fakile, TBWA/Concept, Creative Director

Ranti Atunwa, TBWA/Concept, Executive Creative Director

BRAND	Diageo
ENTRANT COMPANY	digitXplus, Lagos, Nigeria
AWARD	Bronze

Johnnie Walker

Credits

Timilehin Oyedeji, digitXplus, Account Lead

Johnnie Walker

Background

There was a pressing need to re-shape perception around Johnnie Walker being perceived as a "Serious Drink" to a Whiskey that is trendy and can be enjoyed at home with friends and loved ones; whilst also driving recruitment amongst young drinkers.

Creative Idea

Due to the lockdown and restriction in movement, "out of home" activities for our target audience came to a halt, by effect marketing activities. Consumer behaviors and media consumption pattern were automatically influenced.

Our target audience are social and typically would love to hang at a bar with friends but due to the restriction and lockdown all of this was impossible. There was more of home consumption and the brand being a lifestyle brand needs to creatively and tactically breakthrough the clutter as people would typically stick to brands that they know. Also, the time our target audience spent on Television and across digital saw a huge surge, as purchasing behaviour of target audience change – as people purchase items online and got them delivered to them.

We saw an opportunity by leveraging the BBN the biggest reality TV show in Nigeria to drive awareness, affinity, and engagement around Johnnie Walker – driving our in-home bar message "Party Night, Johnnie HighBall"

Strategy

Association on BBN and Johnnie Walker enabled us to contextualize the brand in respect to the need, wants and desires of our TA. We therefore leveraged the Saturday Night Party on BBN to own and drive the conversation around the Johnnie Walker Highball cocktails by customizing cocktails for each housemate and leveraging their influence on their fans.

Execution

With the power of Artificial intelligence, we engaged with fans with real-time response to get actions and reactions around cocktails for their favorite housemate; and each time they talked about their favorite housemate the AI positioned the brand in front of our target audience as we served them personalized message and the house mate's specific cocktail and encourage them to enjoy the party with their Favorite HM buy making their own Highball. It did not end there, it was followed up with personalized DM (Direct Messages to Fans we interacted) with a link to buy the brand online.

Results

The campaign, with the power of Christopher Artificial intelligence, which is real-time delivered 6.1k replies, 763k reach and 17k engagement – meaning that we were able to get the brand in front of people when they express their wants, likes and desire 17k times. We also drove conversations around Johnnie Walker with influencers delivering over 4.3M reach and 9.5M impressions with the #JW80sCandyDance which trended on Twitter.

The party and digital activities (real-time) got our target audience to "sit-up" and enjoy the Saturday Party Night with Johnnie Walker

BRAND   Unilever Ghana - CloseUp

ENTRANT COMPANY   PhD Media, Accra, Ghana

AWARD   Shortlist

Close Up Free to Love Campaign

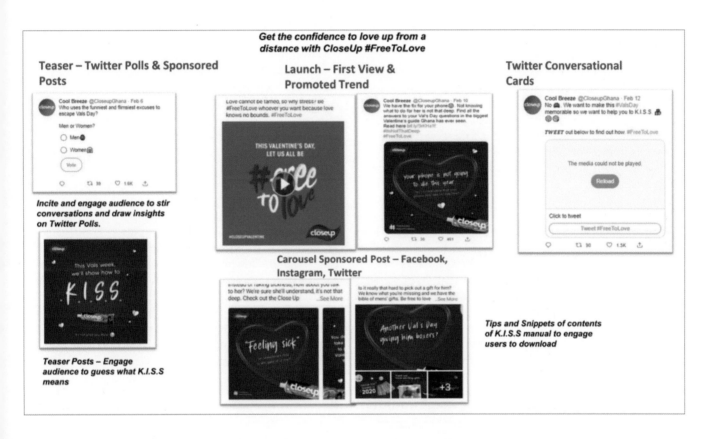

Credits

Raphael Beinamwin, PhD Media Ghana, Associate Director

Charles Nunekpeku, EchoHouse Ghana, Creative Lead

Toyin Osebeyo, DigitXPlus, Implementation Lead

Deborah Eli, PhD Media Ghana, Digital Executive

Close Up Free to Love Campaign

Background

CloseUp empowers consumers to get closer with confidence. However, health and safety measures amidst the COVID'19 pandemic make social distancing key to staying protected. Valentine's day 2021, for CloseUp, was the time to support consumers meaningfully providing the opportunity for them to confidently express their love language from a distance.

The objective was to get users to feel the love and excitement that comes with Valentine's day, with a different approach due to social distancing and other restrictions. Our aim was to increase engagement across all social platforms by providing a KISS (Keep It Super Simple) manual on meaningful ways to spread love and relieve the pressure of Valentine's day and be Free To Love each other.

Creative Idea

The key challenge was to reinforce and sustain CloseUp's communications idea of "the confidence to get closer". With the spike in case counts locally, outings were minimal. It was important to own the conversation on Valentine's Day and also reinforce brand love, beyond having fresh breath to get closer, but also the right strategies and tactics to win the heart of one's admirer or significant other. In the peak of the pandemic, a spike in consumption of digital channels and platforms was observed among all demographics – most especially Gen Y and Gen Z has evolved rapidly. The rise of numerous challenges during national lockdowns, thus providing valuable insights on their receptivity of said campaign – that consumers love to engage and be entertained. It was a rare opportunity and our responsibility to land an impactful campaign that will resonate with our target audience from their phone screens, and put a wide bright smile on the faces of their loved ones.

Strategy

We approached the communications strategy by being relatable, fun, empathic and speaking in a tone that is familiar to the target audience – Gen Z and Gen Y, to gain their trust. Secondly, it was important to go beyond social posts and provide a practical and easy to implement manual for consumers to further emphasis that being free to love should not be as tasking as it seems. Facebook and Instagram posts were heavily promoted, using carousel formats and videos. On Twitter, the use of media polls, encouraged the audience to share previous memorable Valentine's day events and funny excuses their partners gave to avoid the pressure of celebrating Valentine's Day.

Execution

With 1 week to Valentine's Day, it was vital to reach as many people as possible within the short frame of time. A first view and promoted trend was implemented on Twitter – to champion the conversation on celebrating valentine's Day.

Employing the use of multiple posts to generate buzz and anticipation of the release of the KISS manual, ensuring the use of colloquial terms and popular culture trends to drive relevance throughout implementation.

Digital media content based on the "Free to Love" platform was promoted heavily on Facebook, Instagram and Twitter. Driving meaningful engagements online lead, us to deploy First View and Promoted Trend, Conversational Cards and Polls on Twitter. All leading users to download the KISS manual and choose from numerous suggestions on how to make the day special, eliminating the pressure associated with the day.

Results

With just a little over one week of social media activity, the campaign managed to garner 8.8 million impressions across all posts, reaching over 2.3 million users with an average frequency of 3.7 on Facebook and Instagram.

With 15,000 downloads of the KISS manual, and over 59,000 video views generated by Twitter implementation which gained over 898,000 impressions, the physical and emotional gaps, created by the need to stay safe and keep the pandemic under control, were closed up for many. Total engagements obtained across all posts is over 96,000. This campaign earned CloseUp's Free to Love campaign CloseUp the most creative brand award from Twitter.

BRAND   Close Up Ghana
ENTRANT COMPANY   EchoHouse Ghana Limited, Accra, Ghana
AWARD   Campaign Shortlist

Lose Up K.i.S.S. Guide

Credits

Stephen Wong, EchoHouse Ghana Limited, Art Director

Nana Kennedy-Kwofie, EchoHouse Ghana Limited, Lead Copywriter

Ivy Kanda, EchoHouse Ghana Limited, Copywriter

Kweku Yankah, EchoHouse Ghana Limited, Community Executive

Joseph Wristberg, EchoHouse Ghana Limited, Graphic Designer/Motion Graphics

Welbeck Mensah, Freelance, Copywriter

Yousif Abdullah, EchoHouse Ghana Limited, Strategy Director

Millicent Abusah, EchoHouse Ghana Limited, Senior Account Manager

Charles Nunekpeku, EchoHouse Ghana Limited, Account Manager

Lord Tony Adansi, EchoHouse Ghana Limited, Creative Director

Jason Nartey, EchoHouse Ghana Limited, Executive Creative Consultant

Raphael Beinamwin, PHD, Media Account Manager

Lose Up K.i.S.S. Guide

Background

The weeks leading up to Val's Day are always full of anxiety for young lovers who want to do something to impress their partners. The "pressure" is on full blast on social media where young people feel trapped in all this. Couples go through the "Gift Block" a period of not knowing what to get for a loved one. This leads people to ghost their partners, put their phones off on the day, etc. The anxiety was blunting creativity as much as it was not freeing them up to love. The anxiety was going to be even more because it was the first Val's Day in a pandemic. Globally, Closeup's message when it comes to love and relationships, Free To Love. The brand's desire for everyone to be #FreeToLove whoever they choose to be with. Two weeks to Valentine's Day, Closeup Ghana briefed us to let this global line to inspire a Valentine's Day campaign that will be relevant to the Ghanaian audience on social media.

Find a tension that can be broken to set young people free to love

Creative Idea

We decided to run a campaign that will help set people to be #FreeToLove. We wanted to start a conversation and provide a guide that will help them to navigate Val's Day without all the stress and anxiety. Our message was simple: Gifting your loved one isn't that hard if you think about it. It's Not That Deep; Just K(eep) I(t) S(uper) S(imple). A partly irreverent yet helpful take on the subject. From this idea, we created the K.I.S.S. guide, which was done in collaboration with peer opinion leaders from social media in a first of its kind guide that picked no sides, just the side of honest, simple gestures of love

Strategy

Our campaign target was young people - 18 and 35 - who had recently showed interests in Vals day and gifting in their interaction on social media. Guide was made accessible on google drive.

We led with Twitter because of the opportunity it gave us to trigger conversations and also reply people in real time. We planned to deploy first view and the Auto response card. On Instagram, the plan was to run carousel ads that young lovers could relate to. Dark posts were also run to boost our reach and make it easier for the guide to be downloaded.

On Facebook, the plan was to reach as many people as possible with the download link. The plan was also to use selected youth whatsapp groups to also push these ads with the help of peer influencers

GDN ads were also going to be deployed. Finally, we planned to use bulk SMS blasts.

In selecting influencers, we chose people popular for story telling (with twitter threads and then twitter voice note) to make the conversation starters organic.

Execution

Ahead of the release of the guide, the Closeup account started conversations on social media through IG stories but with heavy concentration on twitter where we used tools like polls, twitter threads and voice notes.
We finally released the guide along with artworks that spoke to the different extreme measures people take because of their anxiety over Val's Day.

The document that was circulated alongside catchy and funny copy posts and captions. In a very irreverent, "vals-day-for-dummies" and relaxed tone, the documented highlighted the funny side of these extreme measures. It provided some useful tips on what gift to get a partner, how to plan a stay-at-home date plus some other quirky tit bits. We directly replied & sent DMs of the guide to people who had shown anxiety. The Twitter Auto Response card we deployed made it easier for people to read, endorse and download the K.I.S.S. guide with just an RT!

Our storytellers then presented the guide as a remedy for all the anxiety.

Results

OVER 10000 PEOPLE VIEWED & DOWNLOADED THE KISS GUIDE
- 9.2 MILLION IMPRESSIONS ACROSS DIGITAL
- 6.6 MILLION REACH ACROSS DIGITAL
- 5.6K PAGE VISITS TO THE CLOSE UP ACCUNT
- 58 THOUSAND INTERACTIONS ACROSS DIGITAL
- 59 THOUSAND TWITTER CARD VIDEO VIEWS
- TREND ON VALS DAY
A LOT OF MESSAGES AND THANKS FOR THE GUIDE

Lose Up K.i.S.S. Guide

Don't Ghost Her

Lose Up K.i.S.S. Guide

No More Boxers

Covid-19

BRAND	Cape Verde Government
ENTRANT COMPANY	Mantra Pu, Praia, Cape Verde
AWARD	Shortlist

The Sun

Credits

Júnior Lisboa, Mantra, Creative Director

Júnior Lisboa, Mantra, Copywriter

Ariston Quadros, Art Director

Nenass Almeida, Director

The Sun

Background
Like all countries that have a strong tourist vocation, Cape Verde felt a profound economic impact with the restrictions imposed by Covid-19. On the other hand, surveys indicated that traveling was one of the biggest desires of people in lock-down countries.

Creative Idea
Driven by the need for Cape Verde to become the preferred destination for tourists as soon as possible, the agency created a social media spot for potential visitors. The video addresses, in an unusual way, the feeling of people confined at home, without the possibility of taking a walk on the streets and, even less, traveling. At that time, a simple sunbath was almost impossible for many. For this reason, we put the sun itself to "talk" with people, revealing that it also feels sad to be away from them and inviting everyone to find him in a place where he, in fact, has always been: Cape Verde.

Strategy
The idea was to launch the video on the Government of Cape Verde's profile in Facebook with a segmentation strategy aimed at Cape Verdeans living in Europe and the United States, making them themselves the promoters of the campaign together with their networks of friends. At the same time, we directed the video to people in these same countries with an interest in travel.

Execution
The video was produced entirely at the agency itself, using images from Shutterstock, a volunteer Cape Verdean announcer and footage from the agency itself.

Results
With the Government of Cape Verde fully committed to stop the pandemic that was advancing in a worrying way in the country, the video did not have adequate funding so that it had the expected reach. The successive waves of the pandemic have also postponed its re-launch, which should happen next May 2021.

BRAND   Sanlam
ENTRANT COMPANY   King James Group, Cape Town, South Africa
AWARD   Good

The Olympian

Credits

Alistair King, King James, Chief Creative Officer

Matt Ross, King James, Executive Creative Director

Devin Kennedy, King James, Executive Creative Director

Jared Osmond, King James, Creative Director

Cameron Watson, King James, Creative Director

Kathi Jones, King James, Agency producer

Paul Ward, Giant Films, Director

Martina Shieder, Giant Films, Producer

Nicolaas van Reenen, Field Audio, Sound Engineer

Sean Henekom, King James, Business Unit Director

Jovana Harkhu, King James, Group Account Director

Taryn Walker, King James, Managing Director

Rosemary Boronetti, King James, Stategist

Anthony Lee Martin, Me&My Friends, Editor

Lauren Chavez, King James, Earned Media Specialist

Jade Lotriet, King James, Earned Media Specialist

Simon Kohler, Field Audio, Sound Engineer

Colleen Knox, New Creation Collective, Editor

Riaan Myburg, New Creation Collective, VFX Artist

The Olympian

Background

On the 23rd of March, 2020, South Africa joined the host of myriad other countries and entered a hard lockdown. Next came rumours that the next event and sporting casualty of the pandemic would be the Tokyo Olympic Games. It was in this dismal context that Sanlam aimed to launch a message that encouraged people to hope, with a story that inspired it.

Creative Idea

To launch our new brand platform, Now is the time to plan, Sanlam told the inspirational story of a South African Olympic hopeful. When the Tokyo 2020 Olympic Games were cancelled, Sanlam introduced the world to Caitlin Rooskrantz and the new plan we had given her.

Strategy

As the world shrank for businesses and individuals, trapping us in our homes for weeks then months on end, Sanlam wanted to encourage people to avoid abandoning their dreams altogether, instead refocusing them. If the old plan had gone out the window amidst the pandemic, what was needed, what we wanted to inspire people to, were new plans. This strategy laddered down from the financial human truth that dreams only stand a hope of becoming reality when you actively take steps to achieve them. The creative execution stemmed from this in that we found a story that had one of two endings waiting: either a young Olympian would sit back and watch years of preparation pass without the world getting the chance to see her perform a routine that analyst had tapped for a gold in Tokyo, or she would need another plan to make that dream come true.

Execution

In the lead-up to what would have been the Tokyo Olympic Games, 2020, as sports journalists were discussing what wasn't happening, we told them and the world what was happening. A young South African gymnast was at the centre of the latest Sanlam campaign, and something was coming. We teased the event on our socials, telling more of Caitlin's story in the build-up to the event.

Then, in the context of the CoViD-19 pandemic, we had to work out how to stage an Olympic-level event without an Olympic level production. Or risk to any lives. Every element of the campaign had to embrace the CoViD-19 protocols. Our athlete, Caitlin Rooskrantz, had next to no access to her coaching staff and medical teams. Let alone her rehearsal and training spaces. We had to organise sanitisation of her training spaces, limiting access from outsiders, in order for her to get in the shape necessary to perform. We had to source a location akin to the spectacle of an Olympic stadium, but without a single seated.

Results

A Reach of 184+ million.
2 500 000+ Views
861 000+ Social Engagements.
130 000+ New Visitors to Site.

Credits

Deon van Zyl, Freelance, Director of photography

Darian Simon, Strangelove Studios, Flame Artist

Caitlin Rooskrantz, JGC Gymnastics, Performer

Paul Spiers, New Creation Collective, Editor

Daniel Zoeller, King James, Animator

Emma Drummond, King James, Digital Group Head

Joe Van Schalkwyk, King James, Digital Designer

Liezl Fourie, King James, Digital Designer

Anthony Murray, King James, Retouching Artist

Amy Knight, New Creation Collective, Post Producer

Leticha Kisting, King James, Producer

Miles Davis, King James, Digital Designer

Sue Waters, King James, Campaign Producer

Annemarie Blaensdorf, King James, Project Manager

Rudi Pottas, King James, Project Manager

Emma Rassmussen, King James, Project Manager

BRAND	Stella Artois Africa
ENTRANT COMPANY	King James Group, Cape Town, South Africa
AWARD	Silver

Wet Paint

Credits

Skhumbuzo Tuswa, The King James Group, Group Head Copywriter

Lauren Mitchell, The King James Group, Group Head Art Director

Graeme Jenner, The King James Group, Executive Creative Director

Anna Nashandi, The King James Group, Business Unit Director

Wayne De Lange, Silver Bullet Films, Director

Diana Keam, Silver Bullet Films, Producer

Wet Paint

Background

When lockdown restrictions were eased for the first time in South Africa, people started slipping back into old habits that put their loved ones at risk of COVID-19 infection. People had trouble adjusting to a new way of getting together and they weren't keeping a safe distance from one another. As a social experiment in social distancing, Stella Artois - a brand with a long history of bringing people together - saw an opportunity to use art to help South Africans come together safely at some of the country's busiest public spaces.

Creative Idea

As a mischievous way to help people keep their social distance while in busy public spaces like train stations, bus stops and malls, Stella Artois collaborated with artists to create original artworks that were painted right onto the middle of benches at these locations. A permanent 'Wet Paint' sign was then left there forcing people to keep their distance on either side of the bench, without even knowing they were doing it.

Strategy

The target market is made up of +/- 30 year-old professionals living in urban cities. They strive to achieve a balance between their careers and their desire to spend quality time with the people they care about. Before the pandemic, the brand was running a global campaign titled Together in The Life Artois. In keeping with the times, this changed to 'Together Apart'.

Execution

Stella Artois partnered with two renowned South African artists, Baba Tjeko and Curious Lauren to create art that encouraged social distancing. They created 8 original artworks, which were then painted onto the middle of benches at some of the busiest public spaces in the country.

Each artwork incorporated the artists' iconic styles, while including subtle cues from Stella Artois brand assets.

A high-gloss varnish was applied to the paintings, before a final touch was added - a permanent 'Wet Paint' sign with an invitation for people to sit only on either side of the painting.

Over the next few weeks, people's unconscious change in behaviour was filmed and shared on Stella Artois', as well as the artists' digital platforms as a 'social experiment in social distancing'.

Results

Campaign Film - Over 2,300,000 Views on YouTube
84% Average Percentage Viewed
43% View Through Rate (Benchmark = 34%)
5,000,000 South Africans Reached
26 Pieces of PR Coverage in 1 Month
3:1 Earned Media Value (Benchmark = 1.5:1)

BRAND   Kellogg's
ENTRANT COMPANY   mediaReach OMD, Maryland, Nigeria
AWARD   Bronze

Study From Home With Kellogg's

Credits

Emmanuel Adediran, mediaReach OMD, Media Planner

Jubilee Okuwe, mediaReach OMD, Media Buyer

Wazobia FM & Max, Wazobia FM, Media Partner

Precious Adeleye, mediaReach OMD, Media Planner

Ministry of Education Lagos, Partner

Study From Home With Kellogg's

Background
When the pandemic hit and lockdown was enforced, it came with untold challenges for everyone.

During this challenging time, the majority of brands had shifted their advertising messages to be ones of fears, all sharing similar communication reminding everyone of the dangers of COVID-19 to ensure they stayed home. Whilst these were important messages, Kellogg's wanted to communicate to their young target audience, the children who loved their cereals, and consumer group, the parents, to bring messages of hope and importantly support and normalcy

We knew that for most parents, their number one concern was the disruption to their children's education, and that they were looking for opportunities to help their kids continue to learn, when they were unable to leave the house, and unable to afford gadgets to switch to virtual learning like those in the more expensive private schools who had switched to virtual home-schooling, leaving 80% of school children unable to study further.

Creative Idea
If Kellogg's could own breakfast time, they could facilitate breakfast time learning, ensuring some of the poorest children in Nigeria didn't miss out on crucial learning while been forced into lockdown, something completely out of their control. With no access to laptops or technology to be able to participate in online learning, we turned to traditional media to broadcast their lessons, every day, to keep their brains active, as well as their stomachs full.

Strategy
Kellogg's already knew how to provide the breakfast, we needed to forge partnerships to provide the learning.

In a first of its kind partnership for Nigeria, Kellogg's partnered with the ministry of education, and a leading grassroot media house, Wazobia TV/FM, to introduce a virtual learning programme on TV and Radio for secondary school students. We wanted to keep them busy & active during lockdown, and continue their preparation

for their West African Examination Council (WAEC) assessment. While the government battled COVID-19, we could take one thing off their plates by picking up the reigns of education, and ensuring all children, not just the wealthy, continued to learn during this time.

Execution
We partnered with Min of Education and Wazobia FM, Wazobia TV for the learning program.

Once breakfast had been eaten, we took ownership of segments from 11am – 1pm on radio, Monday to Friday, and 2-4pm on TV, every day. Our lessons gave students the opportunity to study at home with Kellogg's. Giveaways were also tied to the Question & Answer segment, which was a platform that provided Kellogg's with a good opportunity to engage with their target audience and consumers, thereby keeping the brand top of mind during the lockdown period.

To promote the classes, we deployed creatives with high frequency materials such as Logo pop up, Squeeze back and TVC as well as brand mentions in daily tune promos, Hypes and jingles during the programme on Radio during the week with repeats running on weekends. As an extension of this campaign, we gave out scholarships to underprivileged kids in a bid to also alleviate the challenges of the parents whose means of livelihood were also affected.

Results
We reached over 5million of our audience across 3 major states in Nigeria – Lagos, Abuja & Port Harcourt.

We achieved over 5,000 daily engagements and 200 winners throughout the lockdown period. At the end of the examination, rather an overall drop in performance of students this year, WAEC reported a 1% increase over 2019. By being able to truly care for our loyal consumers at a time when it mattered the most, we exceeded our target for the period and grew by 20% at a time when sales for other brand dipped.

BRAND   Marketing Buzz Factor
ENTRANT COMPANY Up In The Sky, Lagos, Nigeria
AWARD   Shortlist

Villains

Credits

Bolanle Akintomide, Up In The Sky NG, Producer/Editor

Jessica Iwayemi, Up In The Sky, Copywriter

Villains

Background

The COVID 19 lockdown had commenced and Nigerians were reported to be disobeying the restrictions and still congregating in large numbers without masks. Our client wanted us to create a video that would compel people to be more mindful about the restrictions.

Creative Idea

The use of children's toys to pass across the idea of COVID 19 germs attacking a body but not being able to spread or increase their numbers because the restrictions were being obeyed.

Strategy

The goal was to create a deliberately amateurish video similar to what children do. The entire nation was in lockdown and the client. encouraging people to obey COVID restrictions and stay home while finding creative outlets of expression.

Execution

The toys were central to the story told with a narration being given by children. We start off with the soldiers planning on how to take over the nervous system and coming to the gradual realisation that their numbers have vastly reduced from when the assault started and that current moment. It shows that over the course of time, there was no way for them to grow in number and infect other people because the COVID 19 restrictions where being followed.

Results

There were quite a number of WhatsApp shares.

BRAND   Mayor of Djougou

ENTRANT COMPANY   Opinion&Public, Abidjan, Ivory Coast

AWARD   Shortlist

Local Solutions Against Global Pandemic

Credits

Kwame Senou, Opinion & Public, PR Counsel

Local Solutions Against Global Pandemic

Background

Like the whole world, Djougou the 3rd most populated city in Benin Republic, was dealing with the COVID-19 pandemic that was depleting its ressources and creating major challenges for the residents of the community and the administration. Unfortunately Benin followed the same approach many governments took which was to have a national response coordinated directly from the capital city with no local direction. The Mayor of Djougou presented the problem to his PR agency that suggested an initiative to influence the government in updating its approach and allocate ressources to the city of Djougou.

Creative Idea

Local Initiatives against Global Pandemic
The idea was to showcase how effectives are local initiatives against a global pandemic that has a lot to do with behavior change. Playing with local and global, was building on the glocal strategy known to the private which the President of Benin Republic and many of his advisers are from.

Strategy

The strategy was to publish an Op-Ed in a major panafrican newspaper to drive a media storm in order to pressure the government of Benin Republic to allocate grants to local communities to fight the pandemic with their local initiatives.
The media selection was done based on the preferred media used by the central government and its various agencies to communicate or publish their press release.

Execution

The Op-Ed was published on Monday, July 13th 2020 by Financial Afrik magazine's website, a leading francophone Africa media that was known to be frequently read by the Finance Minister of Benin who won an award twice from the news outlet. The Op-Ed was then suggested to many beninese media for republishing in order to drive a media storm and was shared across social media on Facebook, WhatsApp and the political WhatsApp groups that are very effective in driving information to the highest levels of the government.

Result

More than 10 media offline and online published the Op-Ed, Key Opinion Leaders shared on their social media. From the Mayor's social media assets, it reached over 20,000 people with organic reach.

Pressured both by the media storm and the need to take immediate action, the central government of the Republic of Benin granted the city of Djougou a special allowance of about USD $150,000 to fight the spread of Covid-19. The success of the action was such that the government instructed other cities and regions in Benin to implement the same strategy, with special grants in excess of 7 millions US$ from the central government.

BRAND   Beiersdorf
ENTRANT COMPANY Carat, Cape Town, South Africa
AWARD   Bronze

Nivea Take Extra Care

Credits

Leila Byrne, Carat, Account Director

Samantha Geyle, The 13th Floor, Creative

Michelle Marialva, The 13th Floor, Creative

Candice Goodman, Mobitainment, Supplier

Nivea Take Extra Care

Background
As one of the world's best-loved personal care brands, NIVEA is all about care and community, even in the face of adversity. When the Covid-19 crisis hit, one of the hardest things was not being able to see vulnerable family and friends, especially elders.

Creative Idea
NIVEA saw an opportunity to do some good by advancing care and community and helping people connect during the initial, isolating stages of the pandemic.

While people stayed at home for the greater good of the community, NIVEA demonstrated their care by giving all South Africans the opportunity to talk to the people they missed the most, sponsored completely by NIVEA.

A system of free 1-minute phone calls enabled people to call their loved ones by dialing a reverse-billed USSD line. These calls gave people the chance to connect and check in with their community and loved ones and South Africa absolutely loved it.

Strategy
NIVEA sponsored the calls and asked for basic demographic information in return, helping the brand build their opt-in database. In order to ensure we built NIVEA's brand awareness, consumers were asked to listen to a 20-second brand message before they could make their phone call.

The real secret to the campaign was the shareability!

When a person received a free call from their loved one, they also received an invitation to make their own free call. Many people shared the opportunity without any prompting. This meant the campaign went viral on the same day it launched!

Execution
We used a combination of social media ads of Facebook, Social Cards on Parent24, Channel24 and W24, and Direct Mobile Marketing via SMS.

A parallel Awareness social media campaign ran at the same time, stressing the importance of hand-washing

Results
This care and community based campaign meant so much to South Africans that on day one alone, 60 000 free calls were made - connecting at least 120 000 South Africans!

By day six 150 000 free calls had been made, putting us 500% over target and connecting 1/4 million people.

NIVEA's database grew by 158 455 opt-in entries - which was a 90% opt-in rate.

The #TakeExtraCare free call campaign reached over 1.2 Million people with a budget of less than R30 000 while the hand-washing element reached 3million people for less than R90 000.

BRAND   Unilever Ghana

ENTRANT COMPANY   PhD Media, Accra, Ghana

AWARD   Bronze

Lifebuoy Ghana DoTheLifebuoy

Reinforcing Lifebuoy's position as the Nation's Hygiene Solution.
#DoTheLifebuoy

Television Executions

Handwash Demo asset in various local dialect – Ga, Twi, Ewe, Hausa, Pidgin, Dagabani, French

Squeeze Back placement on Live telecast of the COVID-19 App Launch, with syndication across 6 other TV platforms

OOH Executions

Handwashing station at Lorry and Bus station before embarkment

Product giveaway to drivers and conductors in bus stations.

Digital Executions

Use of Influencers to drive importance of handwashing in fighting germs using a visual activity called the "Pepper Demo"

COVID Myth Busters on Facebook, Instagram and YouTube

phd

Credits

Raphael Beinamwin, PhD Media Ghana, Associate Director

Esther Laryea, Wild Fusion, Creative Junior Executive

Nana Aba Anamoah, EIB Network, Managing Director

Ezra Oduro, EIB Network – GHONE TV, Media, Account Manager

Kofi Kinaata, Influencer, Artiste

Abena Appiah, PhD Media Ghana, Media Buying Director

Lifebuoy Ghana DoTheLifebuoy

Background

The brand already pursues purpose of saving lives through handwashing agenda but have over the years tailed off due to a lack of activity in promoting this.

COVID'19 pandemic in Ghana gave the brand an opportunity in serving as a frontline brand in fighting the pandemic though education. It also helped through its social good initiative of making product available to the vulnerable in society through creative and innovative media use delivering big impact with limited budget. Ultimately, it pushed the brand to reinforce its position as the Nation's hygiene solution - across the country, ensuring that no one is left behind in the education and protection against the COVID 19 pandemic.

Creative Idea

With a limited budget, the communication strategy took form as a social cause. Pitched partnerships with media houses as the brands way of supporting the fight against the virus to get them on board. We gave out free products that the stations will give out to the vulnerable in society. These products were shared across the country to partner stations who to listeners. All on-air activities were linked with on-ground in community engagement activities being undertaken by the brand which were packaged as news content. Top rated TV and Radio stations joined the campaign as partners thereby massively benefiting from – average discount of 85% was secured for TV, Radio, Influencer mediums. Interestingly, the impact landed the campaign being featured in a music video by one of the country's biggest artist, in collaboration with other orgs for a COVID education music video. Lastly, partnership with the government in the launch of a COVID contact tracing up by being part of the virtual launch.

Strategy

It was important to sustain relevance of Lifebuoy soap during the outbreak of the COVID 19 pandemic.

The distinct changes in consumer behavior in a post-COVID-19 world, TV viewing is likely to increase, likewise web browsing and social media engagement. Additionally, news channels which are seen as the credible source of information in Ghana was already seeing high viewership. Generally, Audiences are making more room for Coronavirus centered contents, rather than regular ads; to aid debunk the numerous conspiracy theories circulating. Our approach was to leverage on using our brand message as a public service announcement in partnership with the Ministry of Health and the Ghana Health Service; thus making us the brand to trust in these times of panic. Consumers were unsettled and panicking, and needed information that could be trusted; amidst the conspiracy theories going round. Finally, to grow brand love amongst consumers to choose Lifebuoy for superior protection against germs.

Execution

Radio - Regional deployment of LIVE PRESENTER MENTIONS during morning and drive time to drive the brand message of washing hands as frequently as possible to stop the spread of the virus.

Digital Media - Sustained the brand presence on Social media with weekly posts to ensure people have enough information; myth debunkers, "spread good habits", "don't spread panic", tips on handwashing, trivia.

OOH – Packs of Lifebuoy soap were given to commuters, public transport drivers to educate them on protecting themselves against germs – due to the nature of their daily routine. Set up handwashing corners in public transport stations to curb spread of virus and build consumer's habit of handwashing throughout the day.

TV – Top 3 National TV stations to reinforce brand as the first choice for protection of germs. Handwashing tutorials in various local dialects to educate the masses pan Ghana. LPMs and Squeeze Back during live coverage of national COVID 19 App Launch.

Results

Within a March – June 2020, Lifebuoy saw an uplift in market share from 4.8% market share In March'20 to 6.5% in June'20.

Digital – Attained a reach of over 7M+ and a reach score of over 65% during the campaign. Influencer led campaign recorded over 600K+ video views on Facebook and Instagram.

BRAND   Venus Tawiah

ENTRANT COMPANY   Now Available Africa, Accra, Ghana

AWARD   Shortlist

Naa Covid-19 Care Campaign

Credits

Emmanuel Amankwah, Now Available Africa, Creative Director

Akwesi Wiredu Agyekum, Now Available Africa, Motion Graphics and Design

Whitney Dena Thompson, Now Available Africa, Senior Social Media Manager

Emeka Dele, Now Available Africa, Media Strategist

Selase Fiakpui, Now Available, Africa Copywriter

Christina Ogoussan, Now Available Africa, Social Media Manager

Collins Owusu-Duku, Now Available Africa, Design and Video Graphics

Constance Afua Mensah, Now Available Africa, Traffic Manager

Naa Covid-19 Care Campaign

Background
The Covid-19 pandemic made 2020 a memorable year for reasons we'd rather forget.
Our lives changed.
Our cities became quiet and empty.
Our countries were locked down …
and our courtesies were replaced with protocols.

Creative Idea
As brand voices, we joined the conversation by doing what we do best.
We used a selection of local and global brands and their position statements to inform Ghanaians about Dos and Don'ts of the pandemic.

Strategy
Our message was received very well across the platforms online (Facebook, Instagram, Twitter, Linkedin, WhatsApp).

Execution
We created a simple GIF with messages which could be shared easily online. This success encouraged us to wrap up the year with another asset that invited Ghanaians to pick up the pieces.
By using brands to tell this story, we stayed true to ourselves and created something memorable
in a year to forget.

Results
25 Million + Total Impressions
2.5 Million + Total Engagement
10% Engagement Rate
28% Ad Recall Rate

BRAND   Godrej group
ENTRANT COMPANY   5ive ltd, NAIROBI, Kenya
AWARD   Shortlist

My Tough is Enough

Credits

Jonah Otieno, 5ive ltd, CEO

Anthony Waithaka, 5ive ltd, Art director

Carol Kuria, 5ive ltd, Account manager

Isaac Lugalia, 5ive ltd, Designer

My Tough is Enough

Background
Pride is a multi-purpose dishwashing liquid that was being pushed during a time when most people were uncertain how things would go with the pandemic.
The brand didn't rank highly amongst the competition as the parent brand wasn't pushing it since it accounted for less than 2% of turnover. However, the Pandemic meant that they needed to create new revenue streams

Creative Idea
Get people to take Pride in themselves by highlighting resilience and toughness rather than the common themes of short lived philanthropy that were happening at the time.

Strategy
We wanted to reach out to people to submit their stories of resilience and highlight that even if we were collectively going through issues, we were picking ourselves up to push on.

Execution
We ran a campaign to get people to submit their stories of resilience during this time and awarded the stories that best demonstrated them all backed by a brand that was left-field when it came to the topic. We chose women and showed them going through the rigors of their day in their spheres of life despite the madness that was going on around them. This ran over a 3 month duration with over 10 million impressions.

Results
We saw an increase in purchase of 40% on the sales, Over 200 stories of resilience submitted, a 49-51% view rate through the duration of the campaign tripling the expectation, 2.6 million views beating the expectation of 600K.

GOOD

For Profit **Organizations**

BRAND   ONEWILDCARD
ENTRANT COMPANY   ONEWILDCARD, Ikeja, Nigeria
AWARD   Shortlist

Gender Permit

Gender Permit

Background

Even in 2020, as a woman, (in most cases) you need to be married to rent an apartment, you need to be accompanied by a man to gain access into some restaurants and pubs, etc.

Gender Permit is a hypothetical product developed to mock our [society's] continued enablement of gender inequality under the guise of 'culture' or 'biological make-up', and create awareness on the need for a truly gender-equal world, where women don't need 'balls' to be treated fairly.

Creative Idea

The idea for the product stemmed from observing and researching how women are often shut down either subtly or blatantly in situations where they have every right to be heard or treated fairly. The message behind it is that women should not have to go that far to be treated fairly and equally.

Strategy

In line with this year's International Women's Day theme #EachforEqual, the message behind Gender Permit helps push gender equality cause closer to its goal. The project shared online on social media platforms and offline via couriers services to women who fight constantly for equal rights, was aimed at sensitising and reminding both men and women of the current state of the world where women are not treated fairly.

Execution

Two days to Women's Day 2020, we delivered some packages containing the Gender Permit and its peripherals to some pioneer women in Nigeria. Online, videos and images were also shared for more awareness. A website was also launched to get the message across to a wider audience.

https://www.onewildcard.com/genderpermit.

Results

The project got positive engagements both offline and online with high numbers of views, engagements and shares.

Credits

Kayode Olowu, ONEWILDCARD, Creative Director

Oyindamola Ogundare, ONEWILDCARD, Art Director

Mariam Omoyele, ONEWILDCARD, Copywriter

Moriam Sulaimon, ONEWILDCARD, Account Manager

BRAND   Sonatel Orange Group
ENTRANT COMPANY   Caractère, Dakar, Senegal
AWARD   Silver

JigeenJangal

Credits

Muriel Kla, Caractère, Executive Creative and Digital Director

Alexandre Julienne, Caractère, Artistic Director

Carole Bordes, Caractere, Copyriwter

Ernesto Hane, Caractere, Chief Innovation Officer

Ndeye Maguette Diawara, Caractere, Offline Project Manager

Mactar Diallo, Caractere, Social Media Manager

Ndeye Rokhaya Diop, Caractere, Online project Manager

Benedicte Samson, Caractere, Digital Factory Executive producer

Ousmane Fall, Challenger, Producer (Films)

Gregory Ohrel, Challenger, Director

seynabou Sarr, Caractere, Copywriter Junior

Aram Beye, Caractere, Community Manager

Ali Diouf, Caractere, Head of strategy

Moussa Boye, Caractere, Media Manager

JigeenJangal

Background
Sonatel Orange Group is the historical operator and leader in Senegal, also present in Mali, Guinea, Guinea Bissau and Sierra Leone. Although the group is very involved in the fields of education, the environment, culture and health through its foundation and its numerous CSR actions, its institutional image reflects its economic success rather than its societal commitment.

Creative Idea
Insight
Every year a girl stays at school, her future earnings increase between 10% to 20%.
In Senegal, girls outnumber boys and have better results at middle school.
But at the University girls make only 40% of total student population due to various social barriers.
Challenge
Commit to keeping girls in school and make Sonatel Orange the Herald of this issue.
Creative idea
Engaging the community through emotion (Film fiction "On the way to school – Format 2mn et 4mn) and sharing experience (Social Experience) broadcasted only on digital). A platform (HumanInsideAfrica.com) that highlights the commitments of Sonatel Group and especially that for keeping girls in school through testimonies and true stories. #JigeenJangal (Girl Learn)

Strategy
Our strategy with this campaign for the «Keeping girls in school» was to encourage it into a more engage Human centric discourse, to tell stories to start the conversation and mobilize in order to (re)position itself as a major player in Social Development.
Media strategy (off and online) : low expenses and a lot of effects.
The campaign's offline media budget (tele-Radio-Press) is less than €40,000. In digital, the media budget is €0. 2 live talks with 5 influencers, who signed up for free, made the film viral and started the conversation.
The first livetalk took place the day before the launch, with the film being shown in preview on a TV set where a representative of the brand to discuss with education specialists. The 2nd Livetalk took place on the day of the launch and triggered many conversations where the #JingeeJangal was widely used: 33 million impressions in less than 10 hours.
Execution
The launch of the campaign took place on the eve of World Education Day with a TV platform sponsored by the brand dedicated to girls' education in Senegal.
On this set the leaders of the group intervened.
The emotional film "On the Way to School" was premiered, launching the conversation around #JigeenJangale. On D-Day (February 24, «World Education Day») the film was broadcast on TV and social media with a call to action inviting people to visit the humaninsideafrica.com platform, listen to the podcasts and share their experiences as well. In radio, we also activated by broadcasting excerpts of podcasts testimonies inviting listeners to connect.
On D+3 a series of stories were broadcast on Facebook and Instagram referring to the web platform. The conversation essentially focused on Twitter with an effective influence strategy.
On D+8 we then activated the second part. That of the experience with the broadcast of the film «testimonials» on our online channels.

Result
A positive, activist and action-oriented digital conversation hailed by all for its relevance and the emotion it generated, the #JiggeenJangal campaign generated an impressive stream of spontaneous testimonies. Young girls, women, but also fathers, brothers, or fellow students told of the barriers, the stops, the injustices, the broken dreams or, on the contrary, the paths of hope and pride that they experienced or crossed. These numerous testimonies opened the way to a change of mentality but also to proposals, Relationships or supportive and inspiring initiatives such as bringing highly educated women into schools to talk to young girls about trades and guidance, etc. The Jigeen Jangale campaign showed the Sonatel Orange group from a new perspective, sharing a unifying, modern and positive vision of society. Its willingness to accompany change with a strong voice was all the more perceived as it was legitimate in view of its long-standing support for girls' schooling, the digital inclusion of women and a gender-sensitive human resources policy. #JingeenJangal has federated speech and demonstrated that a societal and committed momentum can make things happen. As of March 30, 2020, the campaign reached more than 60% of the population in TV and radio and reached over :
- 6,200 mentions of the hashtag ;
- 30,900 interactions ;
- 132 Millions in digital of impressions.

BRAND   Naija 60x60
ENTRANT COMPANY   ONEWILDCARD, Ikeja, Nigeria
AWARD   Shortlist

Speak Truth To Power

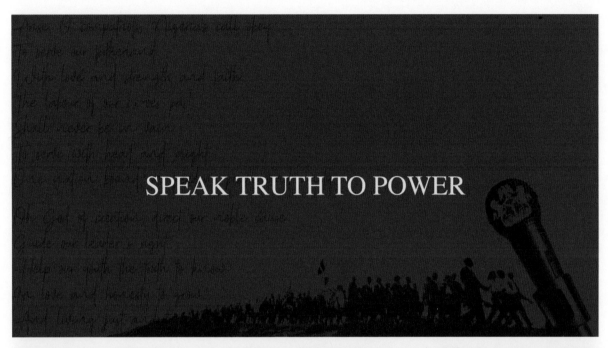

Speak Truth To Power

Background
For too long, Nigerians have lived in inherited silence about the ills that happen in society and by extension, with the government in power. For too long this has reigned, but no more. Now is the time to not only speak up but to speak the truth. For in such truths do we find true freedom.

Creative Idea
To celebrate Nigeria's Independence in 2020, and using spoken word, we called on Nigerians to stand up for what they believe in. For things truly begin to change when we take the necessary actions to get such changes in motion.

Strategy
Placing the spoken word piece against visual images that express Nigeria's history and current reality, we were able to strike a chord in the mind of the viewers. The piece was first aired on IGTV, Instagram, and later on on Twitter as both platforms are used primarily by the younger demographic in Nigeria which is the main target for this wake up call.

Execution
On October 1st, 2020, the video was aired across the brand's active social media platforms and got over a thousand views just on Instagram.

Results
Nigerian social media users at home and in the diaspora engaged with and reposted and/or shared the piece on their personal and group social media platforms.

Credits

Kayode Olowu, ONEWILDCARD, Creative Director

Adeyinka Awe, ONEWILDCARD, Art Director

Kayode Olowu, ONEWILDCARD, Art Director

Adeyinka Awe, ONEWILDCARD, Animator

Oyindamola Ogundare, ONEWILDCARD, Sound Designer

Moriam Sulaimon, ONEWILDCARD, Account Manager

Sage Hassan, Sage Hassan, Word Artist

GOOD

Non-Profit **Organizations**

BRAND   Paradigm Initiative
ENTRANT COMPANY   Up In The Sky, Lagos, Nigeria
AWARD   Silver

Training Day Short Film

Credits

Bolanle Akintomide, Up In The Sky, Producer

Oje Ojeaga, Up In The Sky, Writer

Tolulope Ajayi, Saga City, Director

Muhammad Attah, Since1982, DoP

Uche Nwaohiri, Art Director

Training Day Short Film

Background
Paradigm Initiative wanted to find a more creative dramatic way to bring their 2019 Digital Rights in Africa Report. They approached Up In The Sky turn the facts the report contained into a story the african public would want to watch for its own sake as entertainment and then also learn about the state of digital rights across Africa

Creative Idea
By creating a phantom company as a symbol of african state governments, we use a short film to pass on a usually esoteric message in an NGO's report.

Strategy
Our strategy was to present characters that carried the fears and hopes of the watching public in a deeply emotive way, identification with the characters would drive the strategic intent of the film stronger than anything else we could do.

Execution
The short film dramatizes the growing trend of African governments aggressively taking steps to suppress digital rights of Africans. The film subtly but powerfully expresses how governments and agents of State are increasingly making overt and covert moves to muzzle the voices of Africans online and shows the importance of young people being vigilant and aware of their digital rights. The film is inspired by true events as captured in Paradigm Initiative's Digital Rights Report 2019.

Results
The short film led to more than double the downloads of the 2019 Digital Rights report than in the preceding year. It literally led to an increase in curiosity about if the rights abuses the film showed were true.

BRAND   APAV
ENTRANT COMPANY   Mantra Pu, Praia, Cape Verde
AWARD   Shortlist

Traps

Traps

Background
The pandemic has accentuated unemployment and social inequalities. This environment of hopelessness and despair is even more conducive to human trafficking.

Creative Idea
The creative solution presents a path made with the main arguments used by criminals to attract and convince people to accept their job offers. In fact, real traps that condemn them to a routine of abuse, exploitation and violence.

Strategy
As it is an institution with few financial resources, the agency contributed in the search for partners who could help to expand the campaign. In this sense, the Metro de Lisboa and the Praia City Council provided public spaces to display the posters and also their digital platforms.

Execution
The campaign was totally low cost with layouts using images from Shutterstock. Even the printing of the posters was made possible thanks to the help of a printing partner.

Results
The biggest result was, without a doubt, in reinforcing APAV's image as an institution committed to supporting causes related to human rights.

Credits

Júnior Lisboa, Mantra, Creative Director

Paula Levindo, Mantra, Art Director

Júnior Lisboa, Mantra, Copywriter

BRAND   Project Alert Nigeria
ENTRANT COMPANY   TBWA/Concept, Lagos, Nigeria
AWARD   Bronze

End Rape Campaign

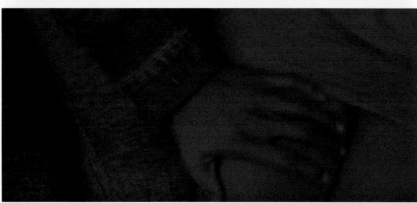

Credits

Wayne Samuel, TBWA/Concept, Copywriter

Chinwe Onuoha, TBWA/Concept, Copy Manager

Alexis Akagha, TBWA/Concept, Account Executive

Biose Isichie, TBWA/Concept, Digital Strategist

Dotun Falade, TBWA/Concept, Digital Strategist

Yusuf Adejumo, TBWA/Concept, Dep. Creative Director

Oyinda Fakile, TBWA/Concept, Creative Director

Ranti Atunwa, TBWA/Concept, Executive Creative Director

End Rape Campaign

Background

The Spotlight Initiative Project is a European Union and United Nations joint global multi-year initiative focused on eliminating all forms of violence against women and girls. The project aim is to focus world attention on this issue and placing it at the centre of efforts to achieve gender equality and women's empowerment.

The Spotlight Initiative Project aims at ensuring that women and girls live a life free of violence and harmful traditional practices. Special focus is on domestic violence, sexual violence.

Creative Idea

In a bid to humanize rape victims, comms often suggest that "It could be your daughter/son", almost as if to say that people are only of value in terms of their relativity to people in society. As such sex workers, mentally unstable (see Jada's entanglement), "loose women" and the downtrodden are not benefactors of the EndRape movement.

Strategy

This execution tackles that saying "First they are humans" and whether they drank that drink, or wore that skirt, or do not elicit sympathy at all, it should not have happened.

Execution

We told the story of a young lady who tried to conform to society's standard in a bid to avoid sexual abuse but ends up getting raped at home.

Results

The campaign surpassed its set targets, gaining the following in 6weeks

2,482,191 IMPRESSION
This is based on how many times the ad was shown on devices this can be repeated multiple times on a device

943,354 REACH
This is measured at the number of individuals the ad was shown to

727,803 POST ENGAGEMENT
This Consists of Likes, Comments, Shares.

1,659,980 VIDEO PLAYS
This consists of all video plays, 3sec – 100% video play

BRAND   Project Alert

ENTRANT COMPANY   TBWA/Concept, Lagos, Nigeria

AWARD   Shortlist

End Rape Campaign

Credits

Wayne Samuel, TBWA/Concept, Copywriter

Chinwe Onuoha, TBWA/Concept, Copy Manager

Alexis Akagha, TBWA/Concept, Account Executive

Biose Isichie, TBWA/Concept, Digital Strategist

Dotun Falade, TBWA/Concept, Digital Strategist

Yusuf Adejumo, TBWA/Concept, Dep. Creative Director

Oyinda Fakile, TBWA/Concept, Creative Director

Ranti Atunwa, TBWA/Concept, Executive Creative Director

End Rape Campaign

Background

The Spotlight initiative through different pillars aim to focus world attention on the issue of violence against women and girls. One of such pillars is educating the community about sexual violence and asking them to speak up against such ills in their communities.

Through the campaign, they intend to Increase engagement on social media, Create awareness around sexual violence and its ills and Educate the communities about sexual violence.

Creative Idea

In a bid to humanize sexual assault victims, comms often suggest that "It could be your daughter/son", almost as if to say that people are only of value in terms of their relativity to people in society.

Strategy

In Neighborhoods, compounds, streets, estates, more care is always given to the infrastructure than to the people that use them. Here we encourage community leaders to embrace and end rape culture as part of their social structure.

Execution

We tell the story of a young couple house-hunting in a posh neighborhood, but even in the cleanest of neighborhoods, there are dirty behaviors we need to get rid of.

Results

over 2million impression, 900,000 reach, 700,000 post engagements in 6weeks.

BRAND   British Deputy High Commission
ENTRANT COMPANY   digitXplus, Lagos, Nigeria
AWARD   Shortlist

She is NOT FOR SALE

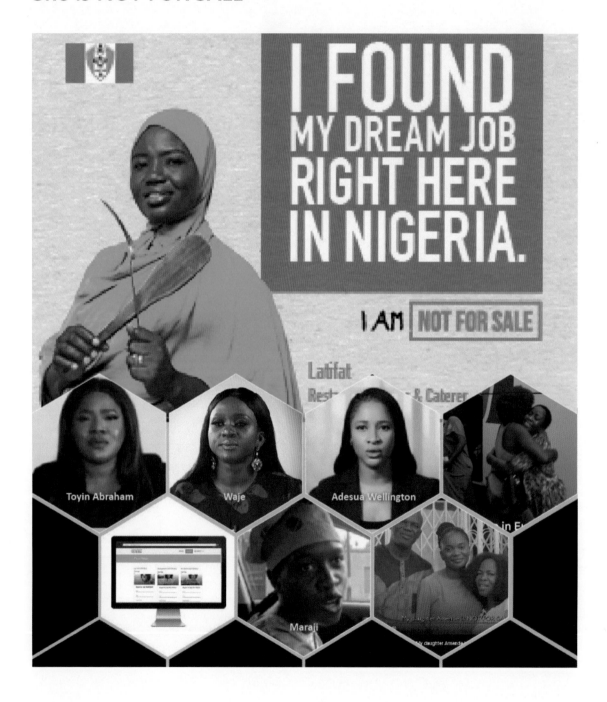

Credits

Toyin Osebeyo, digitXplus, Account Lead

She is NOT FOR SALE

Background
After the Phase 1 of the NOT FOR SALE campaign that promoted positive messages of economic opportunities in Nigeria (focusing on Edo and Delta) to young girls and women between 15-25 years making them aware and discouraging them from getting into human trafficking, while post the campaign many young girls and women have found economic opportunities in Nigeria, the number of human trafficking continued to be on the higher side. The objective of the campaign was to reach vulnerable young girls and women before they become victims, making them aware and to get them to enlist their support in the fight against human trafficking.

Creative Idea
Nigeria is ranked as one of those countries with the highest number of slaves in the world and with 875,000 modern slave victims, Edo State has become infamously known as the country's trafficking hub.

The post campaign analysis and research of the last campaign revealed that the families of these young girls are a major influence in the girls getting into human trafficking. There are still many young women being pressured by their families to travel abroad illegally in an expectation that they will send money home and support the whole family. But, in truth, most women who are sent abroad illegally come home with nothing to show for it. As a matter of haste, they have lost their original investment of travel abroad and wasted years of their early years of life of the young women.

In contrast, there are growing numbers of families that are investing in their daughters for future and being part of their success, hence the message to trigger a strong realization…SHE IS NOT FOR SALE

Strategy
Our focus was Edo and Delta, we identified two set of Target audience
- Primary (parent, older siblings and close relatives of young women)
- Secondary (young women herself).

We carefully selected celebrity influencers from Edo and Delta states
- Waje and Toyin Abraham that catered and reached parents
- Maraji and Adesua that catered and reached young girls and women
Together the 4 had mass appeal and have made a living on their own terms here in Nigeria, to lend their voices to the campaign by discouraging human trafficking.

Execution
The 4 influencers created bespoke content to inform, engage and drive action from the audience.
Additionally, to drive home precision, we had two set of TVCs (using real-life stories, told by young girls and their families), of the family enlisting their support to their daughter deployed on YouTube, Facebook and Instagram targeting Edo and Delta State. To further inspire the target audience, we published online PR articles on top lifestyle blogs and news websites, where our target audience will normally visit for inspiration and encourage them that their daughters' best chance to transform their family's future is here and now in Nigeria. To ensure we captured the audience during their moment of truth, we ran a search campaign by bidding on relevant keywords around human trafficking. The landing page across the various digital channels, was the NOTFORSALE website, in addition to taking the pledge, the website had local opportunities to help them achieve success on their own terms.

Results
The influencers content delivered 1M organic video views, 144K likes and 3.3K comments.
The campaign TVC delivered 128K video views on YouTube, While on Facebook we reached 631K people at an average frequency of 7+.
The campaign delivered 57,500 page views with a 33,800 unique site visits to the NOTFORSALE website to take the Pledge
The comments on the various content across touch points showed that we were able to achieve our strategic proposition, as over 80% of the comments were affirmative.

BRAND   TBWA/Concept

ENTRANT COMPANY   TBWA/Concept, Lagos, Nigeria

AWARD   Bronze

End Sars Campaign

Credits

Wayne Samuel, TBWA/Concept, Copywriter

Kel Nwuke, TBWA/Concept, Art Director

Chinwe Onuoha, TBWA/Concept, Copy Manager

End Sars Campaign

Background
Special Anti Robbery Squad (SARS) is a rogue unit of the Nigeria Police Force with a track record of abusing and harassing young Nigerians. They do this through unlawful marginalization and indiscriminate profiling of the people. Their alleged crimes include extortion, harassment, unlawful arrest, brutality, and even killing.
Fed up with these abuses and the government's failed promises, the youths took to the streets in October 2020 to protest and call for the disbandment of this notorious unit.

Creative Idea
Just like the slogan for the campaign, the creative idea is a clarion call to brands to speak up against police brutality.

Strategy
While the youths risked it all to make their voices heard, there was something else that was very loud- the silence of corporate Nigeria. How do we call out brands without calling them out? We speak their language.

Execution
Brands have a voice- it's in their color, tone of voice, taglines etc. the idea is to speak to them in the language they will understand- their own.

Results
Over 100,000 impressions and 500,000 reach in 1 week. this includes likes, comments, shares etc.

Credits

Biose Isichie, TBWA/Concept, Digital Strategist

Yusuf Adejumo, TBWA/Concept, Dep. Creative Director

Oyinda Fakile, TBWA/Concept, Creative Director

Ranti Atunwa, TBWA/Concept, Executive Creative Director

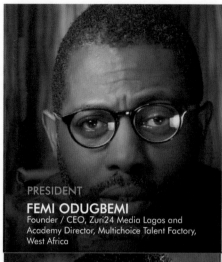

MEET THE ENTERTAINMENT JURORS

PRESIDENT
FEMI ODUGBEMI
Founder / CEO, Zuri24 Media Lagos and
Academy Director, Multichoice Talent Factory,
West Africa

BAMIDELE ARIYO
MD/Chief Creative Officer
Adeptus Advertising, Lagos, Nigeria

VINO SOOKLOLL
CEO & Executive Creative Director
FCB CREAD, Mauritius

KYLE COCKERAN
Creative Director
3verse, Cape Town, South Africa

BADA AKINTUNDE-JOHNSON
Country Manager
ViacomCBS Networks, Africa

AMBOFO SAKIA
Directeur General
Agence Efees, Abidjan, Cote d'Ivoire

COLETTE OTUSHESO
Head Accelerate TV, Lagos, Nigeria

Comic Skits, Entertainment Film, Live Events, Music Video, Sports, Use Of Music

Comic Skits

BRAND   Leadway Pensure PFA

ENTRANT COMPANY ONEWILDCARD, Ikeja, Lagos

AWARD   Bronze

Surecal

Surecal

Creative Idea

Most young people plan on living comfortably in retirement but do not put in the needed work to achieve that. This is why SureCal was created; a financial guide and forecast that steers users in the right direction with respect to current saving habits and life after retirement. The skit was created to express this with some humour, and was shared on social media.

Execution

Targeted at the Nigerian youth, the skit was shared on both the comedian's (Mr. Macaroni) Instagram and the brand's social media platforms. These helped create more awareness for the product and more visits to the brand's website.

Credits

Kayode Olowu, ONEWILDCARD, Creative Director

Mariam Omoyele, ONEWILDCARD, Copywriter

Moriam Sulaimon, ONEWILDCARD, Account Manager

Debo Adebayo, Mr. Macaroni, Art Director

Debo Adebayo, Mr. Macaroni, Production

BRAND   MTN Nigeria
ENTRANT COMPANY TBWA/Concept, Lagos, Nigeria
AWARD   Shortlist

Nepa

Credits

Wayne Samuel, TBWA/Concept, Copywriter

Kel Nwuke, TBWA/Concept, Art Director

Chinwe Onuoha, TBWA/Concept, Copy Manager

Blessed Onwuka, TBWA/Concept, Account Executive

Alexis Akagha, TBWA/Concept, Account Executive

Nepa

Creative Idea
We wanted to tell a relatable story that shows how limitless you can be when they've got reliable data.

Execution
When it comes to taking care of kids, we know most African men score below average. So what happens when one of such men finds himself home alone with his toddler? Using a popular comedian, we were able to tell this hilarious story.

Credits

Yusuf Adejumo, TBWA/Concept, Dep. Creative Director

Gbemi Aleke, TBWA/Concept, Dep. Account & Strategy Director

Oyinda Fakile, TBWA/Concept, Creative Director

Ranti Atunwa, TBWA/Concept, Executive Creative Director

Entertainment **Film**

BRAND   Paradigm Initiative
ENTRANT COMPANY   Up In The Sky, Lagos, Nigeria
AWARD   Bronze

Training Day

Credits

Bolanle Akintomide, Up In The Sky, NG Producer

Oje Ojeaga, Up In The Sky, Writer

Tolulope Ajayi, Saga City, Director

Muhammad Attah, Since1982, DoP

Uche Nwaohiri, Art Director

Training Day

Creative Idea
By creating a phantom company as a symbol of african state governments, we use a short film to pass on a usually esoteric message in an NGO's report.

Execution
The short film dramatizes the growing trend of African governments aggressively taking steps to suppress digital rights of Africans. The film subtly but powerfully expresses how governments and agents of State are increasingly making overt and covert moves to muzzle the voices of Africans online and shows the importance of young people being vigilant and aware of their digital rights. The film is inspired by true events as captured in Paradigm Initiative's Digital Rights Report 2019.

BRAND   Accelerate TV
ENTRANT COMPANY   Accelerate TV, Victoria island, Nigeria
AWARD   Shortlist

Shade Corner

Shade Corner

Creative Idea

The Shade Corner is a talk show that discusses millennial issues and interests in Nigerian society that stem from the increasing divergence of tradition. The topics of each episode tackle Nigerian norms (both good and bad), lifestyle choices, socio-economic challenges and other pressing issues relevant to millennials.

Every episode is anchored by regular hosts but features an influencer, celebrity or media personality who is relevant to the discussion or has been identified as someone with a strong opinion on the topics.

Execution

Every episode is shot at a studio with a uniform set, that is similar to that of a daytime talk show e.g. the view, the ellen show etc.

Each host has contrasting differences in personality from the next to ensure wholesome and wholistic views are shared.

Each episode presents a new topic on which each host, along with the guest are to weigh in on.

Credits

Colette Otusheso, Accelerate TV, Executive Producer

Chidinma Igbokweuche, Accelerate TV, Producer

Adeshola Adreigbigbe, Accelerate TV, Director

Akah Nnani, Accelerate TV, Creator

BRAND   Accelerate TV

ENTRANT COMPANY   Accelerate TV, Victoria Island, Nigeria

AWARD   Bronze

Off The Menu

Credits

Colette Otusheso, Accelerate TV, Executive Producer

Bardia Olowu, Contagious Collective, Creator

Colette Otusheso, Accelerate TV, Creator

Off The Menu

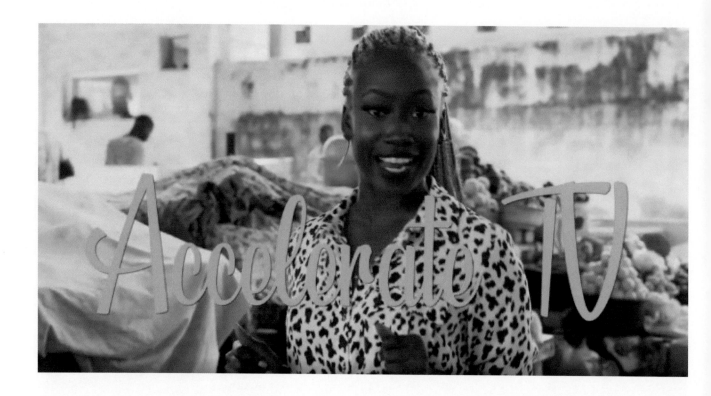

Creative Idea

Off The Menu is a digital show that marries two things the Nigerian audience is passionate about - our celebrities and our food. The show recreates native dishes, with a modern (and sometimes western) twist, showing the audience how to tone down certain flavours, use tricky African spices and encourages everyone who watches to be comfortable in the kitchen.

Each episode features a Nigerian celebrity that has in someway contributed to Nigerian and African pop culture, over the last 15 - 20 years. Guest appearances fromBeverly Naya, Tu Face, Sound Sultan, Kemi Adetiba, Denrele are made throughout the 11-episode season.

Our target audience was people aged 18-35 who are active across all major social media platforms. The majority of our marketing resources were used for digital advertising on Facebook, Youtube and Instagram. Featured guests promoted the episodes on which they appeared.

Execution

Design elements: Luxury kitchen with bright light and neutral tones and colours.
Style: Minimalist with only essential props being used in each episode
Methods/process: interview style, talk show with a cooking activity.

BRAND   Accelerate TV

ENTRANT COMPANY   Accelerate TV, Victoria island, Nigeria

AWARD   Gold

Streets of Lagos

Credits

Colette Otusheso, Accelerate TV, Executive Producer

Lawrence Adejumo, Accelerate TV, Producer / Director

Creative Idea

Streets Of Lagos is a docu-series that takes us into the lives of the every day people with untold stories in different communities in Lagos. Oftentimes, Lagos is portrayed as a bustling West-African city, full of industry and opportunity and different hustles. Lagos is seen as a progressive city, where lifestyle, food, fashion and entertainment are dominant. But what about the people who are less privileged and keep things going through their odd jobs and alternative lifestyles? Streets Of Lagos tells stories of people who are surviving and those who came from nothing and are now thriving.
Target Audience: ages 18-35.

Execution

Each episode featured a guest with a unique story and different point of view of what living in Lagos is like for people in underserved communities.

Each guest was interviewed about his or her life, struggles and aspirations and showed viewers what a typical day in their life is like.

Each episode touched on the aspirational influence of the city and how despite the carnivorous nature of Lagos, each guest was determined to leave their own mark on Lagos through their alternative lifestyles.

Live **Events**

BRAND　　　　　　　　　Diageo: Guinness
ENTRANT COMPANY　　Carat, Cape Town, South Africa
AWARD　　　　　　　　　Silver

Guinness: Night Football Goal Challenge

Credits

Megan Piatti, Carat South Africa, Account Management

Alex Miururi, Carat Kenya, Account Management

Nduku Wamakau, EABL Diageo Kenya, Client

Elan Davidson, Moving Tactics, Live Event Coordinator

Guinness: Night Football Goal Challenge

Creative Idea

Guinness has had an association with football across Africa for decades. To elevate this association, Guinness teamed up with Man United legend, Rio Ferdinand to further entrench its football association. To extend this association we created Guinness Night Football - Football like you have never seen before - a series of heart-thumping consumer events. For the ultimate event of the series in Kenya, with just two weeks to go before the Lagos finale - Guinness took things to the next level, by sourcing global OPTA data through our partner, Goal.com and DAZN. This data source has almost every premier global football move ever made mapped out in GPS like accuracy.

Execution

Together with OPTA and Goal.com we sourced and then virtually mapped out some of the finest goals from players. Guinness then video mapped the path of each goal onto a projected pitch and indestructible goal screen, setup in an impressive space at a popular bar in Kenya. This resulted in a first of its kind tech innovation in Africa, pushing the boundaries of media innovation in the Kenyan market. Fans that indulged in the Guinness Trophy serve through our sales promotion on the night, were eligible to enter the ultimate Guinness Goal Challenge, and were prompted to re-create these legendary goals in front of all the patrons at Greenspot Bar. The digital goal screen was able to record to the millimetre where the ball hit the screen – making for a nail-biting competition for fans that were brave enough to test their skills and a high energy experience for spectators that watched in anticipation.

Credits

Wanjiru Murage, EABL Diageo Kenya, Client

Sara Sandholm, Diageo: Guinness, Client

Graham Deneys, Carat South Africa, Strategist

Megan Sayle, Carat South Africa, Strategist

BRAND   Sanlam
ENTRANT COMPANY   King James Group, Cape Town, South Africa
AWARD   Grand Prix

The Olympian

Credits

Alistair King, King James, Chief Creative Officer

Matt Ross, King James, Executive Creative Director

Devin Kennedy, King James, Executive Creative Director

Jared Osmond, King James, Creative Director

Cameron Watson, King James, Creative Director

Kathi Jones, King James, Agency producer

Paul Ward, Giant Films, Director

Martina Shieder, Giant Films, Producer

Sean Henekom, King James, Business Unit Director

Jovana Harkhu, King James, Group Account Director

Taryn Walker, King James, Managing Director

Rosemary Boronetti, King James, Stategist

Anthony Lee Martin, Me&My Friends, Editor

Lauren Chavez, King James, Earned Media Specialist

Jade Lotriet, King James, Earned Media Specialist

Simon Kohler, Field Audio, Sound Engineer

Colleen Knox, New Creation Collective, Editor

The Olympian

Creative Idea
To launch our new brand platform, Now is the time to plan, Sanlam told the inspirational story of a South African Olympic hopeful. When the Tokyo 2020 Olympic Games were cancelled, Sanlam introduced the world to Caitlin Rooskrantz and the new plan we had given her. And on the 2nd of August, 2020, 10am, the exact date and time she would have performed in Tokyo, we made her the only Olympian to perform in 2020.

Execution
In the lead-up to what would have been the Tokyo Olympic Games, 2020, as sports journalists were discussing what wasn't happening, we told them and the world what was happening. A young South African gymnast was at the centre of the latest Sanlam campaign, and something was coming. We teased the event on our socials, telling more of Caitlin's story in the build-up to the event. Then, in the context of the CoViD-19 pandemic, we had to work out how to stage an Olympic-level event without an Olympic level production. Or risk to any lives. Every element of the campaign had to embrace the CoViD-19 protocols. Our athlete, Caitlin Rooskrantz, had next to no access to her coaching staff and medical teams. Let alone her rehearsal and training spaces. We had to organise sanitisation of her training spaces, limiting access from outsiders, in order for her to get in the shape necessary to perform. We had to source a location akin to the spectacle of an Olympic stadium, but without a single seated

Credits

Nicolaas van Reenen, Field Audio, Sound Engineer

Deon van Zyl, Freelance, Director of photography

Darian Simon, Strangelove Studios, Flame Artist

Caitlin Rooskrantz, JGC Gymnastics, Performer

Paul Spiers, New Creation Collective, Editor

Daniel Zoeller, King James, Animator

Emma Drummond, King James, Digital Group Head

Joe Van Schalkwyk, King James, Digital Designer

Liezl Fourie, King James, Digital Designer

Riaan Myburg, New Creation Collective, VFX Artist

Anthony Murray, King James, Retouching Artist

Amy Knight, New Creation Collective, Post Producer

Leticha Kisting, King James, Producer

Miles Davis, King James, Digital Designer

Sue Waters, King James, Campaign Producer

Annemarie Blaensdorf, King James, Project Manager

Rudi Pottas, King James, Project Manager

Emma Rassmussen, King James, Project Manager

Music **Video**

BRAND MTN Nigeria
ENTRANT COMPANY TBWA/Concept, Lagos, Nigeria
AWARD Bronze

Music Time

Credits

Funmi Ifekoya, TBWA/Concept, Copywriter

Chinwe Onuoha, TBWA/Concept, Copy Manager

Alexis Akagha, TBWA/Concept, Account Executive

Blessed Onwuka, TBWA/Concept, Account Executive

Yusuf Adejumo, TBWA/Concept, Dep. creative Director

Oyinda Fakile, TBWA/Concept, Creative Director

Ranti Atunwa, TBWA/Concept, Executive Creative Director

Music Time

Creative Idea
We wanted to show young Nigerians that the Music Time platform gives them the freedom to be in control- control of their environment, their life, everything.

Execution
Using the freeze technique, we were able to tell this story in a truly interesting and engaging way.

Sports

BRAND Sanlam
ENTRANT COMPANY King James Group, Cape Town, South Africa
AWARD Gold

The Olympian

Credits

Alistair King, King James, Chief Creative Officer

Matt Ross, King James, Executive Creative Director

Devin Kennedy, King James, Executive Creative Director

Jared Osmond, King James, Creative Director

Cameron Watson, King James, Creative Director

Kathi Jones, King James, Agency producer

Paul Ward, Giant Films, Director

Martina Shieder, Giant Films, Producer

Sean Henekom, King James, Business Unit Director

Jovana Harkhu, King James, Group Account Director

Taryn Walker, King James, Managing Director

Rosemary Boronetti, King James, Stategist

Anthony Lee Martin, Me&My Friends, Editor

Lauren Chavez, King James, Earned Media Specialist

Jade Lotriet, King James, Earned Media Specialist

Simon Kohler, Field Audio, Sound Engineer

Colleen Knox, New Creation Collective, Editor

Creative Idea
To launch our new brand platform, Now is the time to plan, Sanlam told the inspirational story of a South African Olympic hopeful. When the Tokyo 2020 Olympic Games were cancelled, Sanlam introduced the world to Caitlin Rooskrantz and the new plan we had given her. And on the 2nd of August, 2020, 10am, the exact date and time she would have performed in Tokyo, we made her the only Olympian to perform in 2020.

Execution
In the lead-up to what would have been the Tokyo Olympic Games, 2020, as sports journalists were discussing what wasn't happening, we told them and the world what was happening. A young South African gymnast was at the centre of the latest Sanlam campaign, and something was coming. We teased the event on our socials, telling more of Caitlin's story in the build-up to the event. Then, in the context of the CoViD-19 pandemic, we had to work out how to stage an Olympic-level event without an Olympic level production. Or risk to any lives. Every element of the campaign had to embrace the CoViD-19 protocols. Our athlete, Caitlin Rooskrantz, had next to no access to her coaching staff and medical teams. Let alone her rehearsal and training spaces. We had to organise sanitisation of her training spaces, limiting access from outsiders, in order for her to get in the shape necessary to perform. We had to source a location akin to the spectacle of an Olympic stadium, but without a single seated

Credits

Nicolaas van Reenen, Field Audio, Sound Engineer

Deon van Zyl, Freelance, Director of photography

Darian Simon, Strangelove Studios, Flame Artist

Caitlin Rooskrantz, JGC Gymnastics, Performer

Paul Spiers, New Creation Collective, Editor

Daniel Zoeller, King James, Animator

Emma Drummond, King James, Digital Group Head

Joe Van Schalkwyk, King James, Digital Designer

Liezl Fourie, King James, Digital Designer

Riaan Myburg, New Creation Collective, VFX Artist

Anthony Murray, King James, Retouching Artist

Amy Knight, New Creation Collective, Post Producer

Leticha Kisting, King James, Producer

Miles Davis, King James, Digital Designer

Sue Waters, King James, Campaign Producer

Annemarie Blaensdorf, King James, Project Manager

Rudi Pottas, King James, Project Manager

Emma Rassmussen, King James, Project Manager

Use of **Music**

BRAND   Leadway Assurance
ENTRANT COMPANY Adeptus Advertising, Lagos, Nigeria
AWARD   Bronze

Camera

Credits

Bamidele Ariyo, Adeptus Advertising, Creative Director

Richard Mgbeokwii, Adeptus Advertising, Art Director

Olushola Oladimeji, Adeptus Advertising, Copywriter

Camera

Creative Idea
This Tv commercial uses music to depict how people go the extra mile for their cars. This plays on a human truth that people especially men, are extra careful and pay very close attention to their cars, they nurture their cars like babies and will go to any extent to ensure the security of the cars.

Execution
The song takes an exciting approach to personify the love and endearments people show towards their cars with a little bit of exaggeration. Playing on this human truth creates the need for insurance thereby asking car owners to subscribe to Leadway Assurance Auto plan. All of this was succinctly communicated through the rich lovey-dovey tune of the music.

For this reason, we created an original soundtrack for the campaign and this was deployed across several touchpoints (radio, digital, TV, and OOH).

Credits

Steve Abaimu, Adeptus Advertising, Copywriter

Babatunde Alaran, Adeptus Advertising, Copywriter

Naomi Oni, Adeptus Advertising, Account Planning

Tolulope Alawode, Adeptus Advertising, Account Planning

BRAND   Budweiser
ENTRANT COMPANY   Isobar Nigeria, Lagos, Nigeria
AWARD   Bronze

Smooth Naija King

Credits

Abena Annan, Client Service

Smooth Naija King

Creative Idea

Digital media has constantly changed the way we create, place and consume content. one thing that has remained constant throughout the years people trust people more than they trust brands.

The task was to use the power of social media to ensure top of the mind awareness for Budweiser as the brewed smooth for Naija kings" using the Budweiser's new brand ambassadors in a way that increases the brand's SOV, build brand equity and generate earned media.

Execution

Leveraging the power of storytelling, social media, influencer and video marketing we themed our campaign –Smooth Naija King . To launch the campaign we created two videos to this effect; one featured a dancer dancing to the smooth soundtrack and cameos from the brand's ambassadors, while the other video featured the brand recently signed suave ex-BBN housemate Mike Edwards, which juxtaposed his smooth mien with closeup shots of Budweiser's golden beer pouring and a pulsating soundtrack repeating the "smooth" phrase to create an unforgettable video that leaves the viewer with one thing; Budweiser is smooth.

The radio ad also featured the same catchy soundtrack making sure anytime you heard the word "smooth" you thought of Budweiser.

Our out of home ads used the brand ambassadors with the same consistent message; "Budweiser is brewed smooth for Naija kings"

BRAND   Suntory
ENTRANT COMPANY   Isobar Nigeria, Lagos, Nigeria
AWARD   Shortlist

King is born

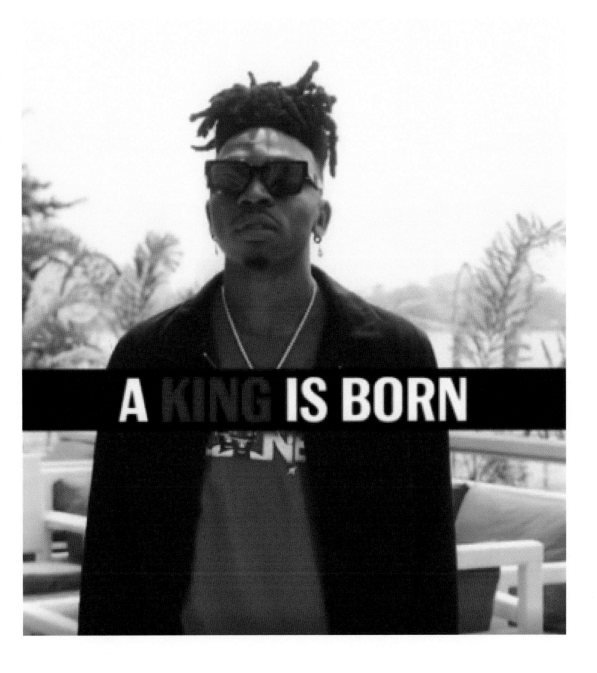

Credits

Abena Annan, Client service

King is born

Creative Idea

Leveraging the power of storytelling, social media, influencer and video marketing we themed our campaign – A King Is Born.

Our story created suspense and hype and left consumers guessing who the new brand ambassadors are. 24 hours before the unveil, we teased our consumers on social media with snippets of the unveil videos asking them to guess who the new brand ambassadors are for a chance to party with them at the unveil party.

We syndicated this piece of content to our existing brand influencers who helped drive the conversation. The day we unveiled; Budweiser dominated the conversation on Twitter for two consecutive days as consumers changed their profile names to #KingBudweiser, #BudweiserXMike, #AKingIsBorn among many others.

The brand also organically trended for 2 days with the following hashtags: #AKingIsBorn, and KingMikeXBudweiser

Execution

Social media has forever changed the way we create, place and consume content. However, one thing has remained the same throughout the years – people trust people more than they trust brands.

With that in mind, Budweiser identified two brand ambassadors who will act as representatives for the brand across multiple platforms.

The task was to use the power of social media to announce to the world Budweiser's new brand ambassadors in a way that increases the brand's SOV For this reason, we created an original soundtrack for the campaign and this was deployed across several touchpoints (radio, digital, TV, and OOH).

BRAND   MTN Nigeria

ENTRANT COMPANY   TBWA/Concept, Lagos, Nigeria

AWARD   Silver

Music Time

Credits

Funmi Ifekoya, TBWA/Concept, Copywriter

Wayne Samuel, TBWA/Concept, Copywriter

Chinwe Onuoha, TBWA/Concept, Copy Manager

Blessed Onwuka, TBWA/Concept, Account Executive

Music Time

Creative Idea
Music your way
We wanted to show young Nigerians that the Music Time platform gives them the freedom to be in control- control of their environment, their life, everything.

Execution
We took advantage of the brand's collaboration with Falz- a popular Nigerian artist and one of the youth's favorites to tell this story.

Credits

Alexis Akagna, TBWA/Concept, Account Executive

Yusuf Adejumo, TBWA/Concept, Dep. Creative Director

Oyinda Fakile, TBWA/Concept, Creative Director

Ranti Atunwa, TBWA/Concept, Executive Creative Director

BRAND   TBWA/Concept
ENTRANT COMPANY   TBWA/Concept, Lagos, Nigeria
AWARD   Bronze

EID Campaign

Credits

Wayne Samuel, TBWA/Concept, Copywriter

Kel Nwuke, TBWA/Concept, Art Director

Yusuf Adejumo, TBWA/Concept, Art Manager

Chinwe Onuoha, TBWA/Concept, Copy Manager

Daniel Kenny, Red Studio, Mastering, mixing, Production

Yusuf Adejumo, TBWA/Concept, Dep. Creative Director

Oyinda Fakile, TBWA/Concept, Creative Director

Ranti Atunwa, TBWA/Concept, Executive Creative Director

EID Campaign

Creative Idea
The creative industry is known for its beef- artist beef artist, actors beef actors, even the ad agencies beef aren't left out. The creative agency decides to take advantage of the last Eid el Adha celebration to preach peace and also show the world their creative prowess.

Execution
It's the season to share beef- well we might as well cook up some.
We created a diss track for other advertising agency. but instead of beefing, we actually praised them.

BRAND Suntory
ENTRANT COMPANY Dentsu McgarryBowen Lagos, Nigeria
AWARD Shortlist

Lucozade Energy to Get Thru it

Credits

Sola Mosuro, Dentsu McGarryBowen Lagos, Creative Director

Lekan Akinyele, Dentsu McGarryBowen Lagos, Deputy Creative Director

Damola Shonubi, Dentsu McGarryBowen Lagos, Senior Art Director

Seye Ogunniyi, Dentsu McGarryBowen Lagos, Senior Copywriter

Juwon Olugboye, Dentsu McGarryBowen Lagos, Account Planner/Strategist

Lucozade Energy to Get Thru it

Creative Idea

TARGET AUDIENCE:
Daily strivers, young adults aged 18 -28 across all sexes. Often on the go, they consider themselves hustlers. Having an innate desire to progress and succeed, they lead full and busy lives, need constant energy and look to products that can complement their natural energy.

CREATIVE IDEA: "Energy to Get Thru It."
The unstable economic, social and political situation in the country meant that Nigerian consumers always had something that represented a pain point to them—something they needed help (extra energy) getting through. From the traffic to the bad roads, the corruption and frustration from all sides.

While as a brand we could not solve all the problems facing our target audience in reality, we positioned ourselves as a brand that gives that extra energy that is needed to get through frustrating, tiring, and draining situations.

Execution
Using relatable, everyday scenarios to bring our message to life, we explored a range of tiring situations that our consumers typically experience daily and showcased the role of the brand in helping them get through it.

Music is a big part of the everyday Nigerian culture.
For this reason, we created an original soundtrack for the campaign and this was deployed across several touchpoints (radio, digital, TV, and OOH).

Credits

Funke Adekola, Dentsu McGarryBowen Lagos, Business Director

Anuoluwapo Kabiawu, Dentsu McGarryBowen Lagos, Account Manager

Boma Harrison, Suntory, Marketing and Trade Marketing Manager

Essien Ekemini, Lucozade Suntory, Senior Brand Manager

BRAND	Quality Beverages - Local Pepsi reseller
ENTRANT COMPANY	CIRCUS! Mauritius, Moka, Mauritius
AWARD	Gold

Pepsi 2020 Film

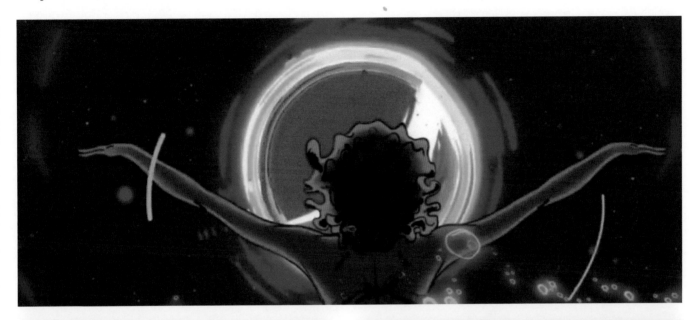

Credits

Vincent Montocchio, CIRCUS!, Executive Creative Director

Gareth Pretorius, CIRCUS!, Creative Director

Karen Pretorius, CIRCUS!, Client Service

Romain Cotegah, CIRCUS!, Art Director

Danitza Vithilingem, CIRCUS!, Producer

Jordan Chamary, CIRCUS!, Producer

Pepsi 2020 Film

Creative Idea

Mauritian youth, under the influence of Western trends, are losing touch with their roots, perceiving our local heritage as old, boring and irrelevant. Pepsi, the longstanding champion of individuality and culture in Mauritius wanted to breath new life into Sega, our fondest and oldest tradition. By updating it's music, fashion, dance and art, we helped it rise into a renewed relevance for the year 2020 through the stylistic approach of Maurifuturism, the inclusion of elements from all of our diverse cultures (African, Indian, European, Chinese) and the refreshing lens of a Pepsi bottle.

The project was delivered to the public through a 360 campaign, the main elements of which were a music video and behind the scenes, showcasing the fact that the project was 100% locally produced (A rarity for this level of production in Mauritius). These elements were then supported by 20 second animations, billboards, radio and store branding across the island. Most modern music is composed with.

Execution

In order to make a new kind of Sega that was more diverse in composition, we included many of the traditional instruments associated with our multi-cultural lineage: Conga and Bongo drums (Africa), Tabla (India), Battery drum kit (Europe) and Tanggu (China). To give the ensemble an even more progressive sound, we created our own orchestra of upcycled percussive instruments including: Buckets, Bottles, Drums made from barrels and even a Tubulum, all played in the unique 6:8 time signature and mixed together with a strong electronic baseline and traditional vocal ad libs.

Appreciated on both social and main broadcasting channels, the result was something totally new and unique, that shattered through the clutter of our airwaves and made Sega relevant to a new generation.
For this reason, we created an original soundtrack for the campaign and this was deployed across several touchpoints (radio, digital, TV, and OOH).

Credits

Aurelie Bestel, CIRCUS!, Producer

Noah Nany, CIRCUS!, Illustrator

Nadia Sodhoo, CIRCUS!, Animator

Kaushik Saubhans, CIRCUS!, Film Director

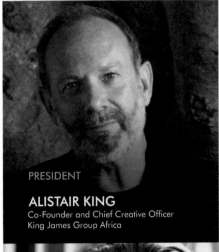

MEET THE HERITAGE JURORS

PRESIDENT

ALISTAIR KING
Co-Founder and Chief Creative Officer
King James Group Africa

VINCENT MONTOCCHIO
Managing Director CIRCUS! Mauritius &
Chief Creative Officer Publicis Groupe Africa

KAYODE OLOWU
Founder/Creative Director
ONEWILDCARD, Lagos, Nigeria

MAX NGARI
Executive Creative Director
Isobar, Nairobi, Kenya

JUNIOR LISBOA
Mindful Owner & Creative Director
Mantra, Praia, Cape Verde

RANTI ATUNWA
Executive Creative Director
TBWA\Concept, Lagos, Nigeria

MURIEL KLA
Executive Creative Director
Caractere, Dakar, Senegal

Audio, Branded Content, Design, Film, Outdoors, Installations & Activations, Print

Audio

BRAND	AIRTEL NIGERIA
ENTRANT COMPANY	Noah's Ark Communications Limited, Lagos, Nigeria
AWARD	Bronze

444

Credits

Lanre Adisa, Noah's Ark Communications Limited, Chief Creative Officer

Bolaji Alausa, Noah's Ark Communications Limited, Executive Creative Director

Maurice Ugwonoh, Noah's Ark Communications Limited, Creative Director

Solomon Osafile, Noah's Ark Communications Limited, Deputy Creative Director

Ezekiel Resedenz, Noah's Ark Communications Limited, Art Director

Maya Adeyemo, Noah's Ark Communications Limited, Art Director

Adetola Shode, Noah's Ark Communications Limited, Art Director

Jesujoba Popoola, Noah's Ark Communications Limited, Copywriter

Judith Ezeali, Noah's Ark Communications Limited, Brand Manager

Abimbola Sanusi, Noah's Ark Communications Limited, Brand Manager

Patience Ugbe, Noah's Ark Communications Limited, Operations

Daniel Akintobi, Noah's Ark Communications Limited, Operations

Adedeji Adeleke, Noah's Ark Communications Limited, Planner

Ife Tabi, Noah's Ark Communications Limited, Planner

Gbadebo, ma lo fo

O je sare lo 4-4-4

O ni. "what for?"

Ma lo go; the code of codes e dey your hand jor

4-4-4, o po, o po. "4" meta, is a meta-4

Okafor, ogini ki jor?

Na Ejiofor you wan recharge for?

No wahala, use 444

Na the code wey sure pass jor

You can recharge your airtime (jor)

You can also subscribe for data (jor, jor, jor)

Direct from source ni o (jor)

4-4-4; that's a meta 4-4-4.

Background

Over the years, Mobile Network services have grown inextricably intertwined with financial services. Although the financial service providers (banks) have always been the ones reaping the benefits of transaction costs with their digital banking solutions such as short codes that enable transactions (buying airtime, data etc) directly from customers' bank accounts. Also, with customer often having multiple bank accounts and consequently, needing multiple short codes, Airtel came up with her own short code, which can singularly help her customers recharge directly from all their bank accounts - *444#

Creative Idea

Creative Idea: "444 is a Meta4" for easy mobile transactions

From the single minded thought, the creative idea naturally leaned towards having fun with the code in itself - 444 being 4 in three places was translated to Meta4 (which when said sounded like a pop-culture-ish/Yoruba way of calling out the code). With the idea settled, it was time for the art itself - a jingle that would make its way to the very top of the Nigerian music scene.
The jingle had to appeal to the "streets", yet appealing to the elites (similar to the naira-marley effect). To cut the long story short, we nailed it and it was an instant hit

Communication Objective

Get the 444 short code to achieved a household level recall among Airtel and non-Airtel users

Business Objective

Increase short code usage by 200% in first 4 weeks of campaign launch

Strategic Approach

With our objectives, two things were clear
We needed high levels of recall
We needed high level of salience (that is people needed to strongly associate *444# with the key service attributes - easy recharge and convenience. Essentially making it a "metaphor" for convenient and easy recharge from bank accounts. Hence our single minded thought; 444 is a metaphor for easy mobile transactions.

Execution

The campaign which was initially designed to be powered by a jingled, ended up being heavily driven by video by popular demand. We created a video for the jingle and ran it in digital channels.

Results

From a business point of view, we totally smashed the targets, where we were required to increase the short code usage by 200% in the first 4 weeks of the campaign, we achieved over 900% increase in first 4 weeks (these are 7 digits figures for context)

The campaign garnered hit reviews and views on various digital platforms. - and reached over 11 million people across Facebook, Twitter, Instagram, and Youtube. As well as over 500,000 engagement instances (likes, comments, retweets, and shares)

The campaign further garnered even more engagement during the Big Brother Naija show, where housemates were required to do their covers - a period where Airtel and 444 were the most talked about subjects in social media

BRAND   CalBank PLC
ENTRANT COMPANY   SMC, Accra, Ghana
AWARD   Bronze

It's Complicated *(Radio Commercial)*

Credits

Sharon Mills, SMC Creative Director & Copywriter

Cyril Alex-Gockel, Mixdown Studio, Production

It's Complicated *(Radio Commercial)*

Ambiance: soft r&b vibes in the background

Girlfriend (calm and smooth): babe, so what are we doing tomorrow…

Guy: Oh…I have to go to the bank…then go and pay for the stuff for my place. Then

maybe back to the bank to transfer what's left to my brother so… [he is cut off]

SFX: Music zips off, Mood switches to African drama with sound effects

Girlfriend (not calm): Are you serious? You're going to the bank TWICE today?

Who is she eh? Which bank? Which branch?

Guy: oh babe but [she cuts him]

Girlfriend (cutting him off): oh don't

babe me…what's her name? teller what…

[Argument fades in the background]
Soundtrack: CalBank soundtrack kicks in

ANNCR: Make your life easy with CalBank Mobile Banking! Just dial *771# and just

like that your life is easy! Transfer money from your CalBank account to any other

accounts, do mobile money and other payments right from your bank account on

your phone! anytime, anywhere! No internet, no charges…it's just that easy! *771#.

Banking is easy with CalBank.

CalBank Forward Together.

BRAND   Anderson Pharmaceuticals
ENTRANT COMPANY TBWA/Concept, Lagos, Nigeria
AWARD   Shortlist

Tropicana Slim

Credits

Wayne Samuel, TBWA/Concept, Copywriter

Oyinda Fakile TBWA/Concept, Creative Director

Ranti Atunwa, TBWA/Concept, Executive Creative Director

SFX. Knocking on door

MVO: That's the sound of your husband's friends unexpectedly showing up at your door

SFX. Metal scraping

MVO: And that's the sound of you finishing everything in your kitchen to feed them

SFX. Sighs, clock ticking, male laughter in the background

MVO: And this, this is you counting the hours till they finally leave

MVO: Terrible isn't it? And that's just your house. Imagine if unwanted guests came visiting your body…

MVO: When you're married to calories, it's only a matter of time before a pot-belly shows up

MVO: Reducing your calorie intake can help avoid such visitors. With Tropicana Slim you can open the door to fat-free sweetness…

SFX. Doorbell rings

MVO: And say welcome to great taste. Tropicana Slim, 0% sugar, 100% sweetness.

BRAND   Green Life Pharmaceutical
ENTRANT COMPANY   TBWA/Concept, Lagos, Nigeria
AWARD   Shortlist

The Hand

Credits

Wayne Samuel, TBWA/Concept, Copywriter

Alexis Akagha, TBWA/Concept, Account Executive

Blessed Onwuka, TBWA/Concept, Account Executive

Chinwe Onuoha, TBWA/Concept, Copy Manager

Yusuf Adejumo, TBWA/Concept, Dep. Creative Director

Mayoyinda Fakile, TBWA/Concept, Creative Director

Ranti Atunwa, TBWA/Concept, Executive Creative Director

The Hand

SFX: Serious, rousing music

MVO: (Serious but charismatic) There's something, about your hands

MVO: It's the way it helped you crawl before you could walk

MVO: The way it gave you support when you could finally stand

MVO: And when doors slammed in your face, what knocked them down?

MVO: It was your hands that opened every window of opportunity

MVO: Nothing has had a hand in your success, more than your own hands!

MVO: (Playful but persuasively) But there's one area your hands may not be fast enough.

MVO: Mosquitos are too small, too sharp, and too smart to be smacked!

MVO: But malaria doesn't have to get out of hand.

MVO: Reach for a box of Lonart, scratch the MAS card at the back, send the revealed code to 38353, wait for confirmation of originality and begin dosage. Scratch it. Confirm it. Take it. With Lonart, you're in safe hands. Lonart contains Artemether and Lumefantrine If symptoms persist after three days, please consult a Doctor.

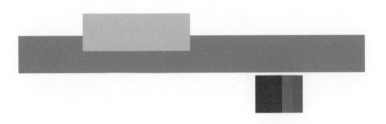

Branded **Content**

BRAND   Sonatel Orange Group
ENTRANT COMPANY   Caractère, Dakar, Senegal
AWARD   Gold

Human In Nature

Credits

Benoit Dorsemaine, Caractère, Artistic Director

Alexandre Julienne, Caractère, Artistic Director

David Vallie,r Caractère, Copywritter

Muriel Kla, Caractère, Executive Creative, Director

Benedicte Samson, Caractère Digital Factory, Executive Producer

Fady Bellot ,Caractère, Community Manager

Mactar Diallo, Caractère, Social media Manager

Ernesto Hane, Caractere, Chief Innovation Officer

Aboulaye Ndao, LayePro Photography, Photography

Ndeye Maguette Diawarra, Caractere, Project Manager

Ndeye Rokhaya Diop, Caractere, Digital project Manager

zeynab Mamoudou, Caractere, Account Manager

BRAND   Ecobank

ENTRANT COMPANY   Takeout Media, Abuja, Nigeria

AWARD   Shortlist

Xpress yourself

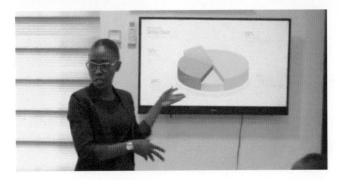

Credits

Elijah Affi, Takeout Media, Creative Director

Miraculous Nwaka, Takeout Media, Content Lead

Michaella Ezima, Takeout Media, Actress

Divine Oforgu, Folkmotion, Director

Faruk Momoh, Folkmotion, Cinematographer

Chris Olunubi, Takeout, Media Actor

Design

BRAND   Guinness Nigeria (Diageo)
ENTRANT COMPANY   Dentsu McgarryBowen Lagos, Ikeja, Nigeria
AWARD   Campaign Silver

Orijin Talk to Nigeria

Loud Speaker

Credits

Sola Mosuro, Dentsu McGarryBowen Lagos, Creative Director

Lekan Akinyele, Dentsu McGarryBowen Lagos, Deputy Creative Director

Lekan Akinyele, Dentsu McGarryBowen Lagos, Illustrator

Damola Shonubi, Dentsu McGarryBowen Lagos, Senior Art Director

Doyin Asagba, Dentsu McGarryBowen Lagos, Copywriter

Funke Adekola, Dentsu McGarryBowen Lagos, Business Director

Anuoluwapo Kabiawu, Dentsu McGarryBowen Lagos, Account Manager

Juwon Olugboye, Dentsu McGarryBowen Lagos, Account Planner/Strategist

Adenike Adebola, Guinness Nigeria (Diageo), Marketing Director

Uche Onwudiwe, Guinness Nigeria (Diageo), Marketing Manager

Noguese Awoniyi, Guinness Nigeria (Diageo), Brand Manager

Orijin Talk to Nigeria

Background

In 2020, Nigeria turned 60 - a landmark event for any country.

For Orijin, as a brand rooted in culture and one that holds the Nigerian heritage dear, this presented a unique opportunity to lead the conversation and celebrate Nigeria. In Nigeria however, due to years and years of corruption, widespread poverty, embezzlement and mismanagement of public funds by the political class as well as the impunity that went with it, nation-wide morale was at an all time low, the sense of patriotism almost totally eroded and replaced with citizen apathy and disenchantment.

Quite frankly, Nigerians were not in the mood to celebrate.

Given the mood in the country, we could neither afford to ignore the reality of our customers nor deliberately contribute to the existing mood by reinforcing negative sentiments.

Creative Idea

We realized that Nigerians are still deeply passionate about their country despite the obvious disenchantment fueled by pent up frustrations and the absence of an avenue to vent, and be heard.

These insights led to the campaign idea "Talk To Nigeria."

Ahead of the Independence Day, we gathered several Nigerians from various walks and gave them the opportunity to address the country as though it were a person.
They had a simple ask: "If Nigeria was a person what would you say to her?"

Strategy

First, we needed to establish the mandatories, the role we want the brand to play, and how we want the brand to be positioned. Our role as a custodian of culture needed to be clear.

Secondly, as a Nigerian brand, we had to step up and find a way to rekindle the spirit of hope in Nigerians and get them to become enchanted with their country again.

With these at the back of our minds, we went back to the consumers to find out a few things.
Interacting with Nigerians, we realized that the lack of excitement about Nigeria @ 60 stemmed from resentment built up over the years.

Deep down somewhere, there was still passionate love for the country. However, present frustrations overshadowed that sense of patriotism. Nigerians had too much to complain about, yet no avenue to air their grief and nobody to hear them.

We realized that Nigerians needed to vent and be heard. They needed a platform to express and channel their emotions.
This led to our Creative Idea, titled "Talk to Nigeria."

Execution

Nigeria is made up of over 200 indigenous tribes, as well as several religions.
To communicate to the entire nation, we thought to do something that everyone could relate with, but which didn't have any strong ties to any one particular tribe.

Using an illustration style that represents Nigerians without being tied to a specific region, tribe or religion, we decided to use the Orijin bottle as the instrument of communication on the execution.

These executions were a part of an entire campaign that also included Video, Print, as well as Digital executions.

Results
• 16,500,000 Impressions.
• 42,000,000 People Reached.
• 17,000 visitors to microsite.
• A further 2,000,000 impressions via influencers and celebrities.

Orijin Talk to Nigeria

Lady

Orijin Talk to Nigeria

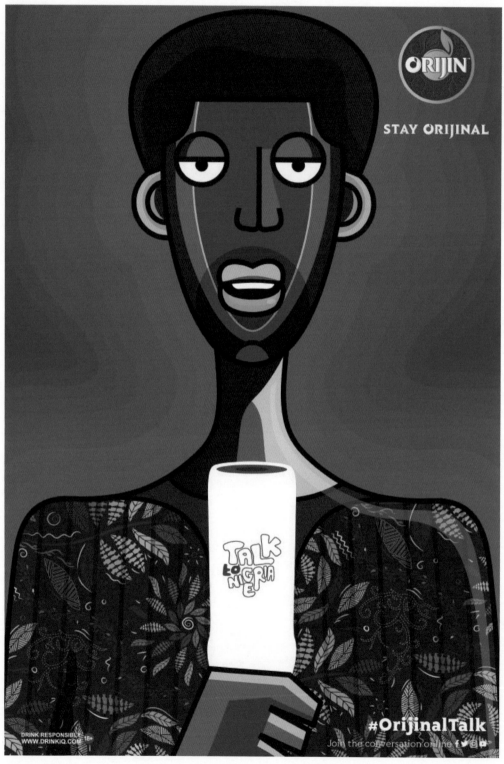

Guy

BRAND   Pizza Jungle
ENTRANT COMPANY   ONEWILDCARD, Ikeja, Nigeria
AWARD   Shortlist

Be Independent

Credits

Doyin Asagba, Dentsu McGarryBowen Lagos, Copywriter

Kayode Olowu, ONEWILDCARD, Creative Director

Mariam Omoyele, ONEWILDCARD, Art Director

Kehinde Owolawi, ONEWILDCARD, Art Director

Mariam Omoyele, ONEWILDCARD, Illustrator

Mariam Omoyele, ONEWILDCARD, Copywriter

Adefunke Afolabi, ONEWILDCARD, Account Manager

Be Independent

Background

Independence is the freedom to choose how to live. To celebrate Nigeria's Independence Day, 2020, we sent forth a reminder that taking control of our lives as a nation and as individuals, is worth it. This is something we should be proud of.

BRAND   Sonatel Orange Group
ENTRANT COMPANY Caractère, Dakar, Senegal
AWARD   Gold

HumanInNature

Credits

Benoit Dorsemaine, Caractère, Artistic Director

Alexandre Julienne, Caractère, Artistic Director

David Vallie,r Caractère, Copywritter

Muriel Kla, Caractère, Executive Creative, Director

Benedicte Samson, Caractère Digital Factory, Executive Producer

Fady Bellot ,Caractère, Community Manager

Mactar Diallo, Caractère, Social media Manager

Ernesto Hane, Caractere, Chief Innovation Officer

Aboulaye Ndao, LayePro Photography, Photography

Ndeye Maguette Diawarra, Caractere, Project Manager

Ndeye Rokhaya Diop, Caractere, Digital project Manager

zeynab Mamoudou, Caractere, Account Manager

Film

BRAND   MALTINA
ENTRANT COMPANY   Noah's Ark Communications Limited, Lagos, Nigeria
AWARD   Bronze

Maltina Variants *(Flavour Quest)*

Credits

Sola Mosuro, Dentsu McGarryBowen Lagos, Creative Director

Lekan Akinyele, Dentsu McGarryBowen Lagos, Deputy Creative Director

Lekan Akinyele, Dentsu McGarryBowen Lagos, Illustrator

Damola Shonubi, Dentsu McGarryBowen Lagos, Senior Art Director

Doyin Asagba, Dentsu McGarryBowen Lagos, Copywriter

Funke Adekola, Dentsu McGarryBowen Lagos, Business Director

Anuoluwapo Kabiawu, Dentsu McGarryBowen Lagos, Account Manager

Juwon Olugboye, Dentsu McGarryBowen Lagos, Account Planner/Strategist

Adenike Adebola, Guinness Nigeria (Diageo), Marketing Director

Uche Onwudiwe, Guinness Nigeria (Diageo), Marketing Manager

Noguese Awoniyi, Guinness Nigeria (Diageo), Brand Manager

Maltina Variants *(Flavour Quest)*

Background

The largest Malt market in Africa and 3rd in the world? That is Nigeria. The Malt brand than had historically led the park? That "was" Maltina. But like most head honchos, threats abound. As such, leading up to 2019 since 2016, the brand had seen a year-on-year decline in market share, and while recovered, was stagnating. As such, we needed to unlock growth. Over indexing among 25 to 34-year-olds who were a relatively small segment of the population, while competing malt brands to whom Maltina was losing market share at the time, had more penetration levels among 18 to 24-year-olds. Something was wrong. However, that was less than half of the story. You see, in Nigeria like most African countries, 18 to 24-year-olds (Life Maximizers) form a significant part of the population.

Brand Objective
Create a youthful affinity for the brand
Dial-up excitement within the category
Grow salience for the brand in the youth segment

Creative Idea

Own The Flavour

This was an idea that suggested the variety of experiences that was out there for the "young explorers" to enjoy, while functionally placing the new flavors of Maltina as the center of consumption occasions for the TG.

Strategy

With our target audience surgically defined, young Nigerians (18 -24-year-old) who were on the cusp of adulthood and independence. Wary of the responsibilities and pressures that come with adulthood, but poised not to lose the joy of experiencing all there was to explore. We called them - "Young Explorers". The plan was to put Maltina, a brand that was previously not on their wavelength, at the center of their exploration (across multiple consumption occasions).

In doing this, however, we created new variants (Pineapple and Vanilla flavors) to appeal to the explorative tendencies of the "young explorers"

Execution

Leading with an impactful OOH and Digital Strategy, we leveraged the power of influencer marketing to drive engagement with this new crop of consumers – the Life Maximizers … the Flavour Geng …

1. To Achieve Broad Reach: we deployed OOH (LEDs, Lampoles & Massive Billboards) & engaging Radio Communication (ROS, Hypes & In-Store Radio) to quickly drive mental availability with the volume target
2. To Achieve Targeted Reach: we dialed up engagement on Digital & Mobile with engaging content from our influencers and UGC from consumers

We supported with TV and PR Amplification to drive Top of Mind and sustenance of the campaign.

Results

Volumes: We delivered +118khl in less than 4 months… (+36% above target) … Delivering a sales uplift of 30% on the total brand….

Consumers Reached: We engaged and sampled over 700,000 consumers across channels

Activations: we executed +100 activations (in Key Accounts, Modern Trade, In Market, Consumer Events, etc)

MEDIA:

OOH: Deployed +518 OOH executions on – LED, Lampoles & Static Billboards

Radio: Deployed 5,069 Spots on Radio with an audience reach of +33.28m through – ROS, Hypes, In-Store Radio engagement, and sponsored programs.

TV: Deployed +620 Spots on Cable, Sponsored programs, In-Cinema Ad Spots, Squeeze backs & on CNN

Digital: Deployed engaging posts, videos, and User Generated Content across FB, IG, Twitter & YouTube …. Delivering +57m Impressions, 16m Unique Reach, 1.4m Engagement (with +17k Reactions) across all platforms combined.

PR Amplification: Reached +58.4m (Paid – 25.3m + Earned – 33.1m) through Print, Blog Posts, UGC from micro-influencers on SoME.

BRAND   Airtel Nigeria

ENTRANT COMPANY   Noah's Ark Communications Limited, Ikeja, Nigeria

AWARD   Shortlist

Airtel Mobile Number Portability *(Tailor)*

Credits

Lanre Adisa, Noah's Ark Communications Limited, Chief creative Officer

Bolaji Alausa, Noah's Ark Communications Limited, Executive Creative Director

Maurice Ugwonoh, Noah's Ark Communications Limited, Creative Director

Solomon Osafile, Noah's Ark Communications Limited, Deputy Creative Director

Adedeji Adeleke, Noah's Ark Communications Limited, Planner

Ezekiel Resedenz, Noah's Ark Communications Limited, Art Director

Maya Adeyemo, Noah's Ark Communications Limited, Art Director

Airtel Mobile Number Portability *(Tailor)*

Background

The Nigerian Mobile Network category has always been one that is quite loose, with customers usually hovering among networks; sometimes having up to 4 sims/network providers at once. Although campaigns and promotional offers, often momentarily dictate which network some customers use per time. This wasn't sustainable for the long term growth that Airtel yearned. In spite of the loose nature of the category, Airtel wanted a switch to her network to be a bit more permanent, so as to generate long term growth. The "million-dollar" question was how?

Creative Idea

Change Your Tailor, Keep Your Swag.

Our creative idea gleaned strongly from the strategy and the consumer research. We brought it closer to home, leveraging the experiences of the target audience by asking - what were those things that people sometimes hold on to for sentimental reasons in spite of the disappointments. Among many examples, "The Tailor " was reverberating, The average Nigerian's experience usually included that one tailor who was so good, but unreliable. And in Airtel fashion, we have a campaign idea - Change Your Tailor, Keep Your Swag - that mirrors the strategy.

Strategy

From our research and client's data, we knew that in spite of the loose nature of the category - where people had multiple sims, category consumers usually had a primary sim that housed the highest chunk of their monthly spend. We knew if we could make Airtel that sim, we could win.
After a series of Focused Group Discussions (FGDs) and surveys, we realized the following
1. Consumers are always open to switching but will rather get a secondary sim.
2. They keep their primary number because it is of sentimental value (usually the first sim they ever had).
3. Even when service may not be the best on their primary sim, the fear of what to expect if they port is what keeps them with all these insights, we knew consumers saw all MNOs as the same, so blowing our trumpets may not be the way to go, rather used this insight to play up the consequence of not porting and benefits of porting to nudge conversion.

Execution

We brought it closer home, leveraging the experiences of the target audience by asking - what were those things that people sometimes hold on to for sentimental reasons in spite of disappointments. Among many examples "The Tailor" was reverberating, The average Nigerian's experience usually included that one tailor who was so good, but unreliable. The campaign was video led, and utilized social media, and television as the main channels

Results

The campaign video garnered hit reviews and views on various digital platforms. - with over 8.6 million views across Facebook, Twitter, Instagram and YouTube. As well as over 76,000 engagement instances (likes, comments, retweets and shares). Online sentiment analysis of the comments and interactions showed 82% positive interactions all across the posts and videos.

On the business side, the number of ported numbers is growing considerably higher than before, with a record breaking projection by the end of the fiscal year.

Credits

Adetola Shode, Noah's Ark Communications Limited, Art Director

Jesujoba Popoola, Noah's Ark Communications Limited, Copywriter

Mayokun Ajayeoba, Noah's Ark Communications Limited, Copywriter

Judith Ezeali, Noah's Ark Communications Limited, Brand Manager

Abimbola Sanusi, Noah's Ark Communications Limited, Brand Manager

Patience Ugbe, Noah's Ark Communications Limited, Operations

BRAND   ARM Pensions
ENTRANT COMPANY   Up In The Sky, Lagos, Nigeria
AWARD   Shortlist

Appreciated TVC

Credits

Bolanle Akintomide, Up In The Sky, Agency Producer

Jessica Iwayemi, Up In The Sky, Copywriter

Tolulope Ajayi, Saga City, Director

Muhammad Attah, Since1982, DoP

Appreciated TVC

Background
The Nigerian Pensions industry has been locked for more than a decade with pension holders not being able to change their pension providers. Under new regulations released in 2020, pension holders could now switch. Our client being a leading provider of pension services was well positioned to make a strong appeal for willing pension holders to switch from their existing providers to ARM Pensions. a company that would truly support their aspirations

Creative Idea
The idea was to use a football players troubled time on a team that would not allow him excel as a parable. Pension holders who were not getting value from their existing providers would see themselves in the travails of the footballer

Strategy

Using colours, football analogies and the crushing disappointment as a backdrop, the strategy was to embed cues that would make the message of switching from other competitors to ARM Pensions unmistakeable.

Execution
Thee coaches are central to the story told - the one who would not give our star a chance and the one that did. The execution was to lift emotion and drop it in equal measure but ensure the story ended on a positive high in a fitting heroes journey.

Results
The film has helped push ARM Pensions to be the second highest net gainers of pension holders switching from other players to ARM.

BRAND   Sonatel Orange Group
ENTRANT COMPANY   Caractère, Dakar, Senegal
AWARD   Grand Prix

JigeenJangal

Credits

Carole Bordes, Caractere, Copywriter

Muriel Kla, Caractere, Executive creative and Digital Manager

Alexandre Julienne, Caractere, Artistic Director

Ernesto Hane, Caractere, Chief Innovation Officer

Ali Diouf, Caractere, Head of strategy

Moussa Boye, Caractere, Media Manager

Arame Beye, Caractere, Community Manager

Mactar Diallo, Caractere, Social Media Manager

Ousmane Fall, Challenger, Producer

Gregory Ohrel, Challenger, Director

Benedicte Samson, Caractere, Digital Factory Executive producer

Ndeye Maguette Diawara, Caractere, Offline Project Manager

Ndeye Rokhaya Diop, Caractere, Online Project Manager

JigeenJangal

Background
Sonatel Orange Group is the historical operator and leader in Senegal, also present in Mali, Guinea, Guinea Bissau and Sierra Leone. Although the group is very involved in the fields of education, the environment, culture and health through its foundation and its numerous CSR actions, its institutional image reflects its economic success rather than its societal commitment.

Creative Idea
Insight
Every year a girl stays at school, her future earnings increase between 10% to 20%. In Senegal, girls outnumber boys and have better results at middle school. But at the University girls make only 40% of total student population due to various social barriers.

Challenge
Commit to keeping girls in school and make Sonatel Orange the Herald of this issue.

Creative idea
Engaging the community through emotion (Film fiction "On the way to school – Format 2mn et 4mn) and sharing experience (Social Experience) broadcasted only on digital). A platform (HumanInsideAfrica.com) that highlights the commitments of Sonatel Group and especially that for keeping girls in school through testimonies and true stories. #JigeenJangal (Girl Learn)

Strategy
We wanted to spark a large conversation around Girls education in the country. This issue needed to be addressed at scale if we wanted to have impact. The cultural context for women is particular in Senegal, many parents accept the idea of putting girls at school but few parents acknowledge the various barriers that hold them behind boys. We needed to show theses barriers and give a voice to women who struggled to have a proper education.

We targeted large public with a national TV spot and created testimonial contents of successful women who had to overcome many obstacles before succeeding. TV and Radio allowed us to reach large audiences and Digital helped us spread various contents (a social experience video, Testimonials, influencers posts, Stories and podcasts of successful women were developed).

Execution
The launch of the campaign took place on the eve of World Education Day with a TV platform sponsored by the brand dedicated to girls' education in Senegal. On this set the leaders of the group intervened. The emotional film "On the Way to School" was premiered, launching the conversation around #JigeenJangale. On D-Day (February 24, «World Education Day») the film was broadcast on TV and social media with a call to action inviting people to visit the humaninsideafrica.com platform, listen to the podcasts and share their experiences as well. In radio, we also activated by broadcasting excerpts of podcasts testimonies inviting listeners to connect. On D+3 a series of stories were broadcast on Facebook and Instagram referring to the web platform. The conversation essentially focused on Twitter with an effective influence strategy. On D+8 we then activated the second part. That of the experience with the broadcast of the film «testimonials» on our online channels.

Results
A positive, activist and action-oriented digital conversation hailed by all for its relevance and the emotion it generated, the #JiggeenJangal campaign generated an impressive stream of spontaneous testimonies. Young girls, women, but also fathers, brothers, or fellow students told of the barriers, the stops, the injustices, the broken dreams or, on the contrary, the paths of hope and pride that they experienced or crossed. These numerous testimonies opened the way to a change of mentality but also to proposals, Relationships or supportive and inspiring initiatives such as bringing highly educated women into schools to talk to young girls about trades and guidance, etc. The Jigeen Jangale campaign showed the Sonatel Orange group from a new perspective, sharing a unifying, modern and positive vision of society. Its willingness to accompany change with a strong voice was all the more perceived as it was legitimate in view of its long-standing support for girls' schooling, the digital inclusion of women and a gender-sensitive human resources policy. #JingeenJangal has federated speech and demonstrated that a societal and committed momentum can make things happen. As of March 30, 2020, the campaign reached more than 60% of the population in TV and radio and reached over :
- 6,200 mentions of the hashtag ;
- 30,900 interactions ;
- 132 Millions in digital of impressions.

TV : 167,8 Gross Rating Point / reach of a campaign : 5 343 945 persons of more than 15 years old

BRAND   Sanlam
ENTRANT COMPANY   King James Group, Cape Town, South Africa
AWARD   Silver

The Olympian

Credits

Alistair King, King James, Chief Creative Officer

Matt Ross, King James, Executive Creative Director

Devin Kennedy, King James, Executive Creative Director

Jared Osmond, King James, Creative Director

Cameron Watson, King James, Creative Director

Kathi Jones, King James, Agency producer

Paul Ward, Giant Films, Director

Martina Shieder, Giant Films, Producer

Sean Henekom, King James, Business Unit Director

Jovana Harkhu, King James, Group Account Director

Taryn Walker, King James, Managing Director

Rosemary Boronetti, King James, Strategist

Nic Apostoli, Strangelove Studios, Colourist

Charmaine Greyling, Strangelove Studios, Flame Artist

Darian Simon, Strangelove Studios, Flame Artist

Caitlin Rooskrantz, JGC Gymnastics, Performer

Paul Spiers, New Creation Collective, Editor

Colleen Knox, New Creation Collective, Editor

Riaan Myburg, New Creation Collective, VFX Artist

Anthony Murray, King James, Retouching Artist

Amy Knight, New Creation Collective, Post Producer

Leticha Kisting, King James, Producer

Daniel Zoeller, King James, Animator

Emma Drummond, King James, Digital Group Head

Joe Van Schalkwyk, King James, Digital Designer

The Olympian

Background

On the 23rd of March, 2020, South Africa joined the host of myriad other countries and entered a hard lockdown. Next came rumours that the next event and sporting casualty of the pandemic would be the Tokyo Olympic Games. It was in this dismal context that Sanlam aimed to launch a message that encouraged people to hope, with a story that inspired it.

Creative Idea

To launch our new brand platform, Now is the time to plan, Sanlam told the inspirational story of a South African Olympic hopeful. When the Tokyo 2020 Olympic Games were cancelled, Sanlam introduced the world to Caitlin Rooskrantz and the new plan we had given her.

Strategy

As the world shrank for businesses and individuals, trapping us in our homes for weeks then months on end, Sanlam wanted to encourage people to avoid abandoning their dreams altogether, instead refocusing them. If the old plan had gone out the window amidst the pandemic, what was needed, what we wanted to inspire people to, were new plans.

This strategy laddered down from the financial human truth that dreams only stand a hope of becoming reality when you actively take steps to achieve them.

The creative execution stemmed from this in that we found a story that had one of two endings waiting: either a young Olympian would sit back and watch years of preparation pass without the world getting the chance to see her perform a routine that analyst had tapped for a gold in Tokyo, or she would need another plan to make that dream come true.

Execution

In the lead-up to what would have been the Tokyo Olympic Games, 2020, as sports journalists were discussing what wasn't happening, we told them and the world what was happening. A young South African gymnast was at the centre of the latest Sanlam campaign, and something was coming. We teased the event on our socials, telling more of Caitlin's story in the build-up to the event.

Then, in the context of the CoViD-19 pandemic, we had to work out how to stage an Olympic-level event without an Olympic level production. Or risk to any lives. Every element of the campaign had to embrace the CoViD-19 protocols. Our athlete, Caitlin Rooskrantz, had next to no access to her coaching staff and medical teams. Let alone her rehearsal and training spaces. We had to organise sanitisation of her training spaces, limiting access from outsiders, in order for her to get in the shape necessary to perform. We had to source a location akin to the spectacle of an Olympic stadium, but without a single seated

Results

A Reach of 184+ million.
2 500 000+ Views
861 000+ Social Engagements.
130 000+ New Visitors to Site.

Credits

Anthony Lee Martin, Me&My Friends, Editor

Lauren Chavez, King James, Earned Media Specialist

Jade Lotriet, King James, Earned Media Specialist

Simon Kohler, Field Audio, Sound Engineer

Nicolaas van Reenen, Field Audio, Sound Engineer

Deon van Zyl, Freelance, Director of photography

Liezl Fourie, King James, Digital Designer

Miles Davis, King James, Digital Designer

Sue Waters, King James, Campaign Producer

Annemarie Blaensdorf, King James, Project Manager

Rudi Pottas, King James, Project Manager

Emma Rassmussen, King James, Project Manager

BRAND   Guinness Nigeria (Diageo)
ENTRANT COMPANY   Dentsu McgarryBowen, Lagos, Nigeria
AWARD   Silver

Orijin Talk to Nigeria

Credits

Sola Mosuro, Dentsu McGarryBowen Lagos, Creative Director

Lekan Akinyele, Dentsu McGarryBowen Lagos, Deputy Creative Director

Funke Adekola, Dentsu McGarryBowen Lagos, Business Director

Juwon Olugboye, Dentsu McGarryBowen Lagos, Account Planner/Strategist

Doyin Asagba, Dentsu McGarryBowen Lagos, Copywriter

Damola Shonubi, Dentsu McGarryBowen Lagos, Senior Art Director

Anuoluwapo Kabiawu, Dentsu McGarryBowen Lagos, Account Manager

Jide Makinde, Technical Magic Media, Director

Joseph Oye, Technical Magic Media, Editor

Uche Onwudiwe, Guinness Nigeria (Diageo), Marketing Manager

Noguese Awoniyi, Guinness Nigeria (Diageo), Brand Manager

Adenike Adebola, Guinness Nigeria (Diageo), Marketing Director

Orijin Talk to Nigeria

Background
In 2020, Nigeria turned 60 - a landmark event for any country.

For Orijin, as a brand rooted in culture and one that holds the Nigerian heritage dear, this presented a unique opportunity to lead the conversation and celebrate Nigeria. In Nigeria however, due to years and years of corruption, widespread poverty, embezzlement and mismanagement of public funds by the political class as well as the impunity that went with it, nation-wide morale was at an all time low, the sense of patriotism almost totally eroded and replaced with citizen apathy and disenchantment.

Quite frankly, Nigerians were not in the mood to celebrate. Given the mood in the country, we could neither afford to ignore the reality of our customers nor deliberately contribute to the existing mood by reinforcing negative sentiments.

Creative Idea
We realized that Nigerians are still deeply passionate about their country despite the obvious disenchantment fueled by pent up frustrations and the absence of an avenue to vent, and be heard.

These insights led to the campaign idea "Talk To Nigeria."

Ahead of the Independence Day, we gathered several Nigerians from various walks and gave them the opportunity to address the country as though it were a person. They had a simple ask: "If Nigeria was a person what would you say to her?"

Strategy
First, we needed to establish the mandatories, the role we want the brand to play, and how we want the brand to be positioned. Our role as a custodian of culture needed to be clear.

Secondly, as a Nigerian brand, we had to step up and find a way to rekindle the spirit of hope in Nigerians and get them to become enchanted with their country again. With these at the back of our minds, we went back to the consumers to find out a few things. Interacting with Nigerians, we realized that the lack of excitement about Nigeria @ 60 stemmed from resentment built up over the years. Deep down somewhere, there was still passionate love for the country. However, present frustrations overshadowed that sense of patriotism. Nigerians had too much to complain about, yet no avenue to air their grief and nobody to hear them.

We realized that Nigerians needed to vent and be heard. They needed a platform to express and channel their emotions.
This led to our Creative Idea, titled "Talk to Nigeria."

Execution
The video and supporting materials were deployed across various mediums, along with a microsite where other Nigerians could join the discourse.

Results
• 16,500,000 Impressions.
• 42,000,000 People Reached.
• 17,000 visitors to microsite.
• A further 2,000,000 impressions via influencers and celebrities.

BRAND   Airtel Nigeria
ENTRANT COMPANY   Noah's Ark Communications Limited, Lagos, Nigeria
AWARD   Shortlist

Know Your Size

Credits

Lanre Adisa, Noah's Ark Communications Limited, Lagos, Nigeria, CCO

Bolaji Alausa, Noah's Ark Communications Limited, Lagos, Nigeria, ECD

Eyo Ekeno, Noah's Ark Communications Limited, Lagos, Nigeria, COO

Know Your Size

Background
Customers have a higher data volume requirement due to the advanced technologies such as LTE, Carrier Aggregation etc; hence, customers need more data to enjoy this experience fully. However, customers are varied and have varying capacity to spend, which is why the Airtel brand was poised at giving different data value options that are within reach for different consumer set.

It is against this backdrop that the agency was tasked with creating a creative communication approach to taking this to market

Creative Idea
The idea was to explore the different data appetites people have and how Airtel has made sure that there's a data plan that fits whatever size of appetite you have or the size of your pocket.

Now you don't have to worry about spending more on a mega plan when what you actually need is a mini- data plan to satisfy your cravings and vice-versa

Strategy
In order to get customers to see data offers as pocket friendly even with the advancement in technology, the agency sought to show that with Airtel, you get different data packages that suit your data lifestyle and financial status.

Execution
TV and Radio spots showing different scenarios in which people wanted something they thought was out of their reach, be it a fitness goal or a luxury hotel room, and them finding out there was a way, within their reach, to get what they wanted were created. These were positioned as metaphors for the different data packages for different pocket sizes which Airtel offered.

Credits

Maurice Ugwonoh, Noah's Ark Communications Limited, Lagos, Nigeria, CD

Judith Ezeali, Noah's Ark Communications Limited, Lagos, Nigeria, BM

Abimbola Sanusi, Noah's Ark Communications Limited, Lagos, Nigeria, BM

BRAND Quality Beverages (Pepsi local reseller)
ENTRANT COMPANY CIRCUS! Mauritius, Moka, Mauritius
AWARD Silver

Pepsi 2020 Film

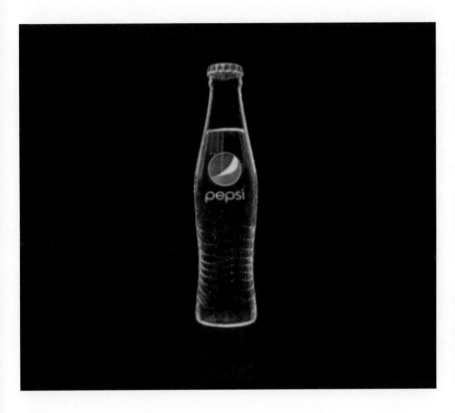

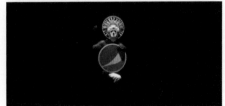

Credits

Vincent Montocchio, CIRCUS!, Executive Creative Director

Gareth Pretorius, CIRCUS!, Creative Director

Karen Pretorius, CIRCUS!, Creative Director

Romain Cotegah, CIRCUS!, Art Director

Danitza Vithilingem, CIRCUS!, Producer

Aurelie Bestel, CIRCUS!, Producer

Jordan Chamary, CIRCUS!, Producer

Noah Nany, CIRCUS!, Illustrator

Nadia Sodhoo, CIRCUS!, 2D Animator

Kaushik Soubans, CIRCUS!, Film Director

Jean Christophe Ah Seng, CIRCUS!, External Production Manager

Pepsi 2020 Film

Background
Mauritius is a fairly conservative Island in the middle of the Indian ocean, a melting pot of multi-cultural diversity with the lineage of it's inhabitants coming from Africa, India, Europe and China. 5 years ago, the we launched the MWA MO KONTAN campaign in Mauritius. (Literally: I don't care what you think, I just love it), leaving aside the likes of Britney Spears and Kendall Jenner and instead choosing to localise the brand, positioning it close to the hearts of the Mauritian youth, by supporting their desire to break taboos and social norms and live life on their own terms.

Today Mauritian youth, under the influence of Western trends, are losing touch with their roots, perceiving our local heritage as old, boring and irrelevant.

Creative Idea
Pepsi, the longstanding champion of individuality and culture in Mauritius wanted to breath new life into Sega, our fondest and oldest tradition. By updating it's music, fashion, dance and art, we helped it rise into a renewed relevance for the year 2020 through the stylistic approach of Mauri-futurism, the inclusion of elements from all of our diverse cultures (African, Indian, European, Chinese) and the refreshing lens of a Pepsi bottle.

Strategy
We approached the refresh of our traditional culture by making it something that we could own and be proud of as a people, rather than simply westernising it. The entire project was conceived, developed and produced 100% locally (a rarity for a production of this scale), heroing a myriad of local talent from animators and illustrators to engineers, choreographers and musicians ,through the creation of Sega Music video with a modern twist and a behind the scenes showcasing how the project brought local talent together. The project was delivered to the public through a 360 campaign, the main elements of which were a music video and behind the scenes, launched on both social and main broadcast channels, these elements were then supported by 20 second animations for each Pepsi variant, billboards, radio and store branding across the island.

Execution
We chose to refresh Sega, our fondest and oldest tradition: its music, its dance, its fashion, its art. And embrace our diversity through Afro-futurism, Indo futurism, Chino futurism and Western futurism to create a unique blend: Mauri-Futurism!

In order to make a new kind of Sega Music that was more diverse in composition, we included many of the traditional instruments associated with our multi-cultural lineage: Conga and Bongo drums (Africa), Tabla (India), Battery drum kit (Europe) and Tanggu (China). To give the ensemble an even more progressive sound, we created our own orchestra of upcycled percussive instruments including: Buckets, Bottles, Drums made from barrels and even a Tubulum, all played in the unique 6:8 time signature and mixed together with a strong electronic baseline and traditional vocal ad libs.

The wardrobe, make-up and styling again draw reference from traditional Sega outfits, with the added inclusiveness of influence from both traditional and progressive A

Results
The Campaign was a massive success, with a unanimously positive online reaction and an unusually deep penetration into social engagement amongst the digitally savvy percentage of our population.

53% of Mauritian facebook users reached

34, 328 - engagements

18 600 - 1 minute views

42.3 x more comments
31.1 x more shares
and 23.1 reactions
than a usual pepsi post

BRAND   Wema Bank Plc
ENTRANT COMPANY   Wema Bank Plc, Lagos, Nigeria
AWARD   Shortlist

The Future of Banking

Credits

Funmilayo Falola, Wema Bank Plc, Head, Brand and Marketing Communications Dept.

Akintunde Marinho, Utopia Media, CEO

Morolake Philips-Ladipo, Wema Bank Plc, Project lead

Abisola Smith, Wema Bank Plc, Team Lead, Digital Marketing Unit

BRAND   Hacey Foundation
ENTRANT COMPANY   Noah's Ark Communications Limited, Lagos, Nigeria
AWARD   Gold

Stop Female Genital Mutilation

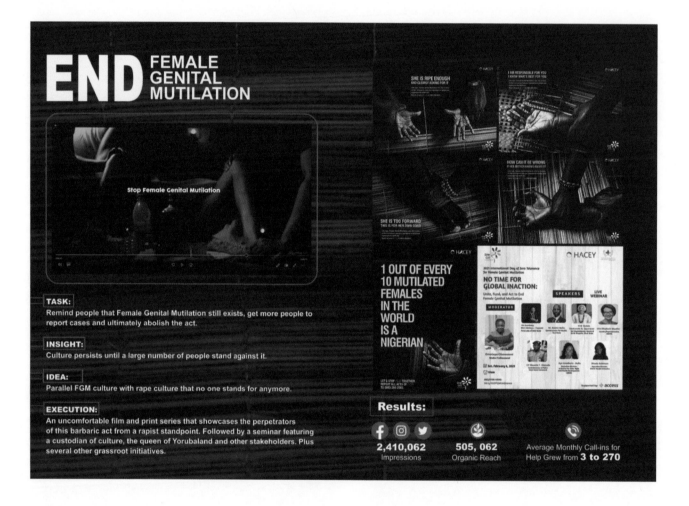

Credits

Lanre Adisa, Noah's Ark Communications Limited, Lagos, Nigeria, CCO

Bolaji Alausa, Noah's Ark Communications Limited, Lagos, Nigeria, ECD

Eyo Ekeno, Noah's Ark Communications Limited, Lagos, Nigeria, COO

Maurice Ugwonoh, Noah's Ark Communications Limited, Lagos, Nigeria, CD

Gabriel Olonisakin, Noah's Ark Communications Limited, Lagos, Nigeria, AD

Yekeen Ibrahim, Noah's Ark Communications Limited, Lagos, Nigeria, AD

Kazeem Lawal, Noah's Ark Communications Limited, Lagos, Nigeria, AD

Jumoke Akinyele, Noah's Ark Communications Limited, Lagos, Nigeria, BM

Stop Female Genital Mutilation

Background

The mutilation of the female genitals is a despicable act committed on females, not only in Nigeria, but in several other countries; both African and Non- African. With no known benefits, this act further has a snowball effect on the self-esteem, health and the life of women.

Although, in Nigeria, there's a law called the VAPP Act that makes FGM a punishable act, it has not been implemented by all states and convictions via this act are few and far between.

With this FGM being especially prevalent in Nigeria, with 1 out of every 10 mutilated women in the world being NIgerian, we needed to call attention to the menace that has long since gone unchecked.

It is against this backdrop, that the agency chose to develop an awareness campaign which would aid in dissuading people from committing this act.

Creative Idea

The idea was to call out the similarity between FGM and another act which always hits close to home, Rape. The idea was born out of the insight that there are other ways to rob a girl child of innocence and life's pleasures besides just rape; one of which is female genital mutilation. This was done to bring the act of FGM closer to people so that they can understand just how bad FGM is for women and how, like rape, it is an infringement of women's right and thus, is punishable by law.

Strategy

In partnership with hacey, the strategy guiding this campaign was to get people to know about the absurdity and existence of FGM in a way that would get the perpetrators to stop doing it and the bystanders to take an active stand against it .

Execution

We used a series of chilling, horror-themed visuals and stories to draw public attention to the gravity of FGM as compared to rape and child trafficking.

Prints and videos showing female body parts forcefully being held down by male hands were created. With copies calling out the similarities between the act of Rape and FGM, people were urged to also be proactive in curbing the act by lobbying their lawmakers into implementing the VAPP act and to report any acts of FGM they see being committed.

Credits

Maria Omole, Noah's Ark Communications Limited, Lagos, Nigeria, BM

Ojumi Olufade, Noah's Ark Communications Limited, Lagos, Nigeria, BM

Jesujoba Popoola, Noah's Ark Communications Limited, Lagos, Nigeria, CW

Mabayomejie Akinyemi, Noah's Ark Communications Limited, Lagos, Nigeria, CW

Segun Odejimi, Noah's Ark Communications Limited, Lagos, Nigeria, CW

Patience Ugbe, Noah's Ark Communications Limited, Lagos, Nigeria, Operations

Daniel Akintobi, Noah's Ark Communications Limited, Lagos, Nigeria, Operations

BRAND   Builders Warehouse
ENTRANT COMPANY   King James Group Johannesburg, Johannesburg, South Africa
AWARD   Silver

Human Nature

Credits

Janet Booysen, Builders Warehouse, Marketing Executive

Jacques du Preez, Builders Warehouse, Creative Manager

Roshana Burnett, Builders Warehouse, Content Manager

Jean Ochse, Builders Warehouse, E-commerce Executive

Nokwethemba Mthetwa, Builders Warehouse, Social Media Coordinator

Deidre Coetzee, Builders Warehouse, Marketing Planning Manager

Graeme Jenner, King James, Executive Creative Director

Michael Wilson, King James, Creative Director

Graeme Jenner, King James, Art Director

Michael Wilson, King James, Copy Writer

Human Nature

Credits

Lebo Levuno, King James, Client Service

Kathi Jones, King James, Head of Broadcast

Sue Tyler, King James, Producer

Claire Fyfe, Easy Solve Solutions, Editor

Gui Felix, Easy Solve Solutions, Online editor

Ettienne Bosch, Easy Solve Solutions, Animator

Elben Schutte, Pressure Cooker Studios, Music

James Matthes, Pressure Cooker Studios, Music

Neil Leachman, Pressure Cooker Studios, Sound Design

James Matthes, Pressure Cooker Studios, Sound Design

BRAND   Project Alert
ENTRANT COMPANY   TBWA/Concept, Lagos, Nigeria
AWARD   Shortlist

Spotlight Initiative

Credits

Wayne Samuel, TBWA/Concept, Copywriter

Chinwe Onuoha, TBWA/Concept, Copy Manager

Alexis Akagha, TBWA/Concept, Account Executive

Kel Nwuke, TBWA/Concept, Art Director

Yusuf Adejumo, TBWA/Concept, Dep. Creative Director

Oyinda Fakile, TBWA/Concept, Creative Director

Ranti Atunwa, TBWA/Concept, Executive Creative Director

BRAND	Godrej Group
ENTRANT COMPANY	TBWA/Concept, Lagos, Nigeria
AWARD	Shortlist

My tough is enough

Credits

Jonah Otieno, 5ive ltd, CEO

Anthony Waithaka, 5ive ltd, Art Director

Carol Kuria, 5ive ltd, Account Manager

Isaac Lugalia, 5ive ltd, Designer

Shadrack Kiema, 5ive ltd, Digital Strategist

My tough is enough

Background
Pride is a multi-purpose dishwashing liquid that was being pushed during a time when most people were uncertain how things would go with the pandemic.
The brand didn't rank highly amongst the competition as the parent brand wasn't pushing it since it accounted for less than 2% of turnover. However, the Pandemic meant that they needed to create new revenue streams

Creative Idea
Get people to take Pride in themselves by highlighting resilience and toughness rather than the common themes of short lived philanthropy that were happening at the time.

Strategy
We wanted to reach out to people to submit their stories of resilience and highlight that even if we were collectively going through issues, we were picking ourselves up to push on.

Execution
We ran a campaign to get people to submit their stories of resilience during this time and awarded the stories that best demonstrated them all backed by a brand that was left-field when it came to the topic.

We chose women and showed them going through the rigors of their day in their spheres of life despite the madness that was going on around them. This ran over a 3 month duration.

Results
We saw an increase in purchase of 40% on the sales, Over 200 stories of resilience submitted.

Outdoor, Installations **& Activations**

BRAND — Noah's Ark Communications Limited
ENTRANT COMPANY — Noah's Ark Communications Limited, Lagos, Nigeria
AWARD — Campaign Shortlist

Murder

Murder 1

Credits

Lanre Adisa, Noah's Ark Communications Limited, Lagos, Nigeria, CCO

Bolaji Alausa, Noah's Ark Communications Limited, Lagos, Nigeria, ECD

Eyo Ekeno, Noah's Ark Communications Limited, Lagos, Nigeria, COO

Maurice Ugwonoh, Noah's Ark Communications Limited, Lagos, Nigeria, CD

Mitchelle Dofounga, Noah's Ark Communications Limited, Lagos, AD

Yekeen Ibrahim, Noah's Ark Communications Limited, Lagos, Nigeria, AD

Kazeem Lawal, Noah's Ark Communications Limited, Lagos, Nigeria, AD

Murder

Background

When asked to describe what your mother or a mother figure has been like in your life. You hear people either talk about the tenacity or caring nature or willingness to go to any length for the ones they love and so on.

However, as Africans, there is one thing the majority of us can agree on; the various seemingly 'wicked' acts our mothers commit in a bid to raise us as healthy, well trained, independent individuals. It is against this backdrop the agency created its mother's day ads to celebrate African mothers.

Creative Idea

There's this saying that 'all African parents went to the same parenting school' because of the similarity of their actions. Hence, the agency decided to call out those things in our childhood our mothers did to us that seemed wicked/criminal to us when we were kids but that we can look back at now and laugh.

Strategy

In order to try to bring about that nostalgic feeling and walk down memory lane for both mothers and their children, the agency sought to understand what we as Africans in general can all say 'Yes! My mother did this to me too'.

Execution

A couple images that contained a mother holding her child in seemingly compromising positions were captured. With copies like 'Charge- Attempted Murder, Verdict- Not Guilty', the images sought to show that the ways in which our mothers handled us were all with the best of intentions.

Results

Qualitative metrics such as offline and online talk-ability which are the main results of our campaign are not best captured not by numbers, but from a business perspective, the campaign generated interest in the agency, which led to a number of new business opportunities for the agency.

Credits

Nike Ladokun, Noah's Ark Communications Limited, Lagos, CW

Segun Odejimi, Noah's Ark Communications Limited, Lagos, CW

Mabayomijie Akinyemi, Noah's Ark Communications Limited, Lagos, CW

Jumoke Akinyele, Noah's Ark Communications Limited, Lagos, BM

Maria Omole, Noah's Ark Communications Limited, Lagos, BM

Ojumi Olufade, Noah's Ark Communications Limited, Lagos, BM

Patience Ugbe, Noah's Ark Communications Limited, Lagos, Nigeria, Operations

Murder

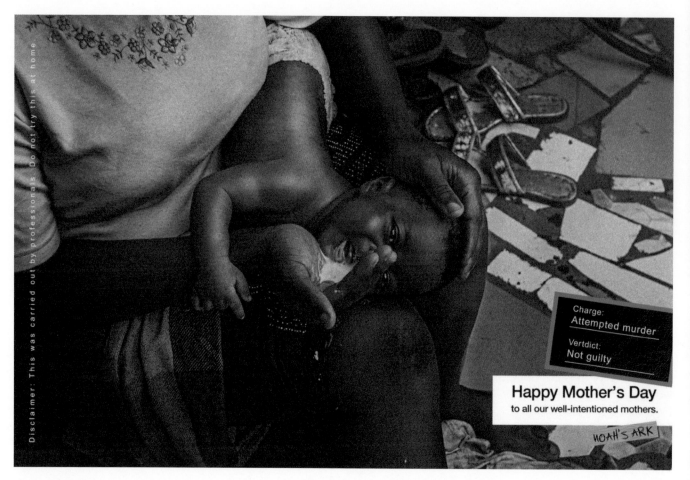

Murder 2

BRAND   Airtel Nigeria
ENTRANT COMPANY   Noah's Ark Communications Limited, Lagos, Nigeria
AWARD   Campaign Grand Prix

Airtel Data is Life

Hardcore Filtered Guys

Credits

Lanre Adisa, Noah's Ark Communications Limited, Lagos, Nigeria, CCO

Bolaji Alausa, Noah's Ark Communications Limited, Lagos, Nigeria, ECD

Maurice Ugwonoh, Noah's Ark Communications Limited, Lagos, Nigeria, CD

Solomon Osafile, Noah's Ark Communications Limited, Deputy Creative Director

Ezekiel Resedenz, Noah's Ark Communications Limited, Art Director

Maya Adeyemo, Noah's Ark Communications Limited, Art Director

Airtel Data is Life

Background

Prior to the Airtel - Data Extension campaign, the mobile data category had an established band for its monthly data plans (1k would give 2GB, etc). However this no longer fit in with the growing data appetite and consumption due to the growing digital space and the capacities of contemporary devices. Nigerians needed more data, and Airtel, being the data centric brand that they are known to be, we needed to start a shift in the category and align our data propositions to the evolving needs of consumers.

Creative Idea

Our creative idea was to show that more data could bring out sides to people that they didn't know they had.

Strategy

People's behaviors tend to change when they have an abundance of something. Our Strategy was to bring to life the potential results of getting more data thanks to Airtel's data extension.

Execution

Our execution centred around showing the softer sides of 'Agberos' (street thugs) that was brought about thanks to access to more data. We showed these so called 'hardcore men' with snapchat filters to drive home the message that there are more sides to people that only more data can bring out.

Results

Since the initial launch of the main campaign in November, Airtel added approximately 2.2 million new customers between the initial campaign launch and February, with a 6.6% increase.

The campaign was also published in the prestigious Lurzer's Archive, generating talkability both online and offline.

Credits

Adetola Shode, Noah's Ark Communications Limited, Art Director

Jesujoba Popoola, Noah's Ark Communications Limited, Copywriter

Mayokun Ajayeoba, Noah's Ark Communications Limited, Copywriter

Judith Ezeali, Noah's Ark Communications Limited, Brand Manager

Abimbola Sanusi, Noah's Ark Communications Limited, Brand Manager

Patience Ugbe, Noah's Ark Communications Limited, Operations

Airtel Data is Life

Hardcore Filtered Guys

Airtel Data is Life

Hardcore Filtered Guys

BRAND   Hacey Foundation

ENTRANT COMPANY   Noah's Ark Communications Limited, Lagos, Nigeria

AWARD   Campaign Bronze

Stop Female Genital Mutilation

Sister

Credits

Lanre Adisa, Noah's Ark Communications Limited, Lagos, Nigeria, CCO

Bolaji Alausa, Noah's Ark Communications Limited, Lagos, Nigeria, ECD

Ekene Eyo, Noah's Ark Communications Limited, Lagos, Nigeria, COO

Maurice Ugwonoh, Noah's Ark Communications Limited, Lagos, Nigeria, CD

Segun Odejimi, Noah's Ark Communications Limited, Lagos, Nigeria, CW

Stop Female Genital Mutilation

Background

The mutilation of the female genitals is a despicable act committed on females, not only in Nigeria, but in several other countries; both African and Non- African. With no known benefits, this act further has a snowball effect on the self-esteem, health and the life of women. Although, in Nigeria, there's a law called the VAPP Act that makes FGM a punishable act, it has not been implemented by all states and convictions via this act are few and far between. With this FGM being especially prevalent in Nigeria, with 1 out of every 10 mutilated women in the world being NIgerian, we needed to call attention to the menace that has long since gone unchecked.

It is against this backdrop, that the agency chose to develop an awareness campaign which would aid in dissuading people from committing this act.

Creative Idea

The idea was to call out the similarity between FGM and another act which always hits close to home, Rape. The idea was born out of the insight that there are other ways to rob a girl child of innocence and life's pleasures besides just rape; one of which is female genital mutilation. This was done to bring the act of FGM closer to people so that they can understand just how bad FGM is for women and how, like rape, it is an infringement of women's right and thus, is punishable by law.

Strategy

In partnership with hacey, the strategy guiding this campaign was to get people to know about the absurdity and existence of FGM in a way that would get the perpetrators to stop doing it and the bystanders to take an active stand against it .

Execution

We used a series of chilling, horror-themed visuals and stories to draw public attention to the gravity of FGM as compared to rape and child trafficking.

Prints and videos showing female body parts forcefully being held down by male hands were created. With copies calling out the similarities between the act of Rape and FGM, people were urged to also be proactive in curbing the act by lobbying their lawmakers into implementing the VAPP act and to report any acts of FGM they see being committed.

Credits

Jesujoba Popoola, Noah's Ark Communications Limited, Lagos, Nigeria, CW

Mabayomijie Akinyemi, Noah's Ark Communications Limited, Lagos, Nigeria, CW

Jumoke Akinyele, Noah's Ark Communications Limited, Lagos, Nigeria, BM

Maria Omole, Noah's Ark Communications Limited, Lagos, Nigeria, BM

Ojumi Olufade, Noah's Ark Communications Limited, Lagos, Nigeria, BM

Patience Ugbe, Noah's Ark Communications Limited, Lagos, Nigeria, Operations

Stop Female Genital Mutilation

Father

Stop Female Genital Mutilation

Mother

Stop Female Genital Mutilation

Guardian

BRAND Red Slate Group
ENTRANT COMPANY Outori Limited, Lagos, Nigeria
AWARD Bronze

Sweet Sixty

Credits

Obinna Aniche, Redslate Group, Group President

Oluwole Olagundoye, Outori Limited, Managing Director

Unekwu Nwaezeapu, Outori Limited, Manager, Business Unit

Seun Ajayi, Outori Limited, Head of Operations

Ayodeji Onabajo, Outori Limited, Head of Business Unit

BRAND   Noah's Ark Communications Limited
ENTRANT COMPANY   Noah's Ark Communications Limited, Lagos, Nigeria
AWARD   Campaign Shortlist

Xenophobia

Credits

Lanre Adisa, Noah's Ark Communications Limited, Lagos, Nigeria, CCO

Bolaji Alausa, Noah's Ark Communications Limited, Lagos, Nigeria, ECD

Maurice Ugwonoh, Noah's Ark Communications Limited, Lagos, Nigeria, CD

Solomon Osafile, Noah's Ark Communications Limited, Deputy Creative Director

Adedeji Adeleke, Noah's Ark Communications Limited, Planner

Xenophobia

Background
Following the ruthless xenophobic attacks on foreign Africans who had migrated to South Africa earlier in the year, a series of events occured which seemed to drive a wedge between South Africans and the rest of Africa; as fellow Africans felt like they were being betrayed and had started to seek revenge. It is against this backdrop Noah's Ark Communications decided to run a campaign showing our stand against xenophobia.

Creative Idea
Following the insight that the xenophobia attacks was suicide in its own right, we sought to show that we (Africans) needed to stop the attacks or we we were only going to harm ourselves.

Strategy
As Africans, it is only sensible that we work and stick together for the betterment of the continent. Hence, any harm we cause to a fellow African, is basically harm to ourselves, In the wake of the xenophobic attacks, the strategy for the #SayNoToXenohobia campaign was to show that the xenophobia attacks were basically us dying by our own hands. Ergo, committing suicide.

Execution
We created various images which portrayed a person each strangling themselves to death with the South African flag as backdrop. This was followed by the copy #SayNoToXenophobia.

Results
Our results are best captured in qualitative metrics such as the talk-ability that was generated both offline and online.
From a business side of things, inquiries into what agency did this by people of interest led to new business opportunities for the agency.

Credits

Sodiq Sheu, Noah's Ark Communications Limited, Art Director

Yekeen Ibrahim, Noah's Ark Communications Limited, Art Director

Mitchelle Defounga, Noah's Ark Communications Limited, Art Director

Nike Ladokun, Noah's Ark Communications Limited, Copywriter

Dunni Elemide, Noah's Ark Communications Limited, Copywriter

Toke Mabayomije, Noah's Ark Communications Limited, Copywriter

Adeola Ogunade, Noah's Ark Communications Limited, Brand Manager

Bidemi Alfred, Noah's Ark Communications Limited, Brand Manager

Anita Erhirhie, Noah's Ark Communications Limited, Brand Manager

Patience Ugbe, Noah's Ark Communications Limited, Operations

Daniel Akintobi, Noah's Ark Communications Limited, Operations

Ife Tabi, Noah's Ark Communications Limited, Planner

Xenophobia

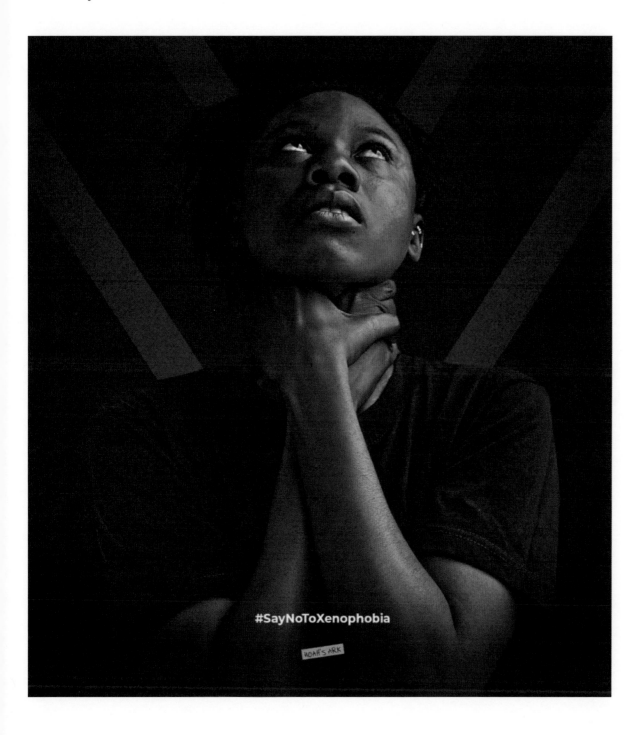

Xenophobia

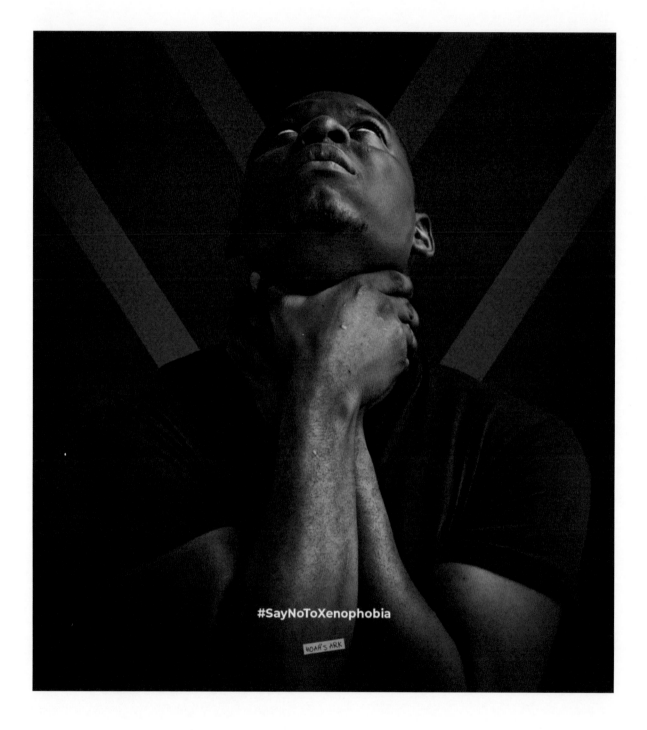

BRAND   Safaricom PLC
ENTRANT COMPANY Dentsu Aegis Network Kenya, Nairobi, Kenya
AWARD   Gold

The Bantering Billboard

Credits

Gideon Ruita, Dentsu Aegis Network-Kenya, Account Director

Alex Tutu, Dentsu Aegis Network-Kenya, Managing Director

Teresa Makori, Dentsu Aegis Network-Kenya, Associate Creative Director

Stuti Ahuja, Safaricom PLC, Brand Manager

Stella Arithi, Safaricom PLC, Brand Manager

Amelia Aganda, Safaricom PLC, Brand Manager

Miriam Waititu, Dentsu Aegis Network-Kenya, Business Unit Head

The Bantering Billboard

Background

Safaricom, the biggest telecommunications company in Kenya, was celebrating their 20-year anniversary and they wanted to make it about making it about their consumers and engaging with their consumers. Their message to Kenyans was two simple words: "Twende Tukiuke", meaning, "Let's go beyond."

So, we set out to bring the message home to each one of them, with a first of its kind out of home execution.

Creative Idea

To mark 20 years of serving Kenyans, Safaricom, Kenya's biggest telecommunications company had one unifying message with two simple words, "Twende Tukiuke", meaning, "Let's go beyond."

To truly live this, they wanted to go above and beyond by including Kenyans in their celebrations in a very personal way.

We used this opportunity to install a campaign that would utilise the flexibility of DOOH with the dwell time and we came up with a digital billboard that would not only interact and draw the attention of our audience.

Strategy

First using Google Mobility reports, we were able to identify Nairobi's busiest round about that would offer us the ample dwell time to run our execution. We then used KURA (Kenya Urban Roads Authority) data to identify the peak traffic hours where we could engage with motorists stuck in traffic.

Execution

We installed a camera on the digital screen at the University Way round about facing inbound traffic. The Camera, using AI and machine learning was able to identify the make colour and model of the vehicles and customise a shout out to the motorists based on the above metrics projected on the screen. The message on the screen also broke down what "Kiuke" meant to Kenyan commuters and in the end asked them to hoot twice or give a response to engage with us.

Results

Over the course of 8 weeks, we were able to serve over 28000 unique messages and were able to reach a peak of 58k Impressions daily from the interaction with the screen thereby truly harnessing the power of an offline platform in delivering online traction, talk-ability and measurable results.

BRAND   Saudabel

ENTRANT COMPANY   3Verse, Cape Town, South Africa

AWARD   Campaign Shortlist

Live Happy Side Up

Credits

Ivan Johnson, 3Verse, Executive Creative Director

Kyle Cockeran, 3Verse, Creative Director

Peni Buckton, 3Verse, Art Director

Kat Jonas, 3Verse, Art Director/Copywriter

Matt Bayly, 3Verse, Head of Art

Richard Meissenheimer, 3Verse, Finished Art

Seymour Lottering, 3Verse, Traffic/Art Buying

Live Happy Side Up

Background
Saudabel, Angola's premier water brand, was facing increased market competition, and, after 20 years as the nation's iconic water, was in need of a refresh.

Creative Idea
It's only when you turn the trademark Saudabel® water drum upside down that you get to enjoy all the fresh, wholesome, purity and vitality inside. A sight synonymous with Saudabel for more than 20 years.

Strategy
Middle to upper income Angolans, corporates and expatriates were the targets in this campaign - the idea being to refocus consumers on Saudabel's iconic status in Angola, using its trademark 5-gallon flip-barrel as the impetus for the campaign.

Execution
We took a selection of people from our typical target market and depicted them enjoying themselves in their everyday lives - but turned the shots upside down... a reference to the fact that the bottle itself has to be turned upside down in its 5-gallon dispenser unit in order to be used and enjoyed.

Results
Orders: up 62%. Spontaneous Awareness: up 24.5%. Website Traffic: up 48%.

Credits

Ray Kippie, 3Verse, Production

Joanne Stone, 3Verse, Client Service

Brittany Priest-Jones, 3Verse, Client Service

Kay Orlandi, 3Verse, Strategy

Andrew Alexander, 3Verse, Managing Partner

Sheila Stiller, Saudabel, Managing Director

Eckhard Stiller, Saudabel, Managing Partner

Claire Tanner-Roberts, 3Verse, Senior Copywriter

Live Happy Side Up

Live Happy Side Up

★ Judges' Note: This execution included the new 3-gallon drum packshot, echoing the parent and child in the picture.

BRAND   Mauvilac Industries Ltd
ENTRANT COMPANY   CIRCUS! Mauritius, Moka, Mauritius
AWARD   Campaign Silver

Mauvilac Thousands

Thousand of Mauritian Greens

Mauvilac Thousands

Background

Mauritius is well known for its colourful houses which is reminiscent of the diverse cultural background of its people coming from all around the world. Mauvilac is a 100% Mauritian paint brand that creates colours inspired by the colourful island.

Creative Idea

Opening a paint bucket is an invitation to indulge in the Mauritian life. A simple dip of the brush brings forth the colours and magic of our beautiful and colourful island. Inside a pot we have everything to get Mauritius in colour.

Strategy

December being the full summer and festive season where people are very often on holidays, it is well known that this is the time when Mauritians are eager to have their houses painted to welcome the festive season and the new year. The campaign was launched during that festive period.

Execution

The making of these artworks were made possible thanks to the use of photomontage using 3D , illustration and photography. The artistry in the making of it required a lot of time and eyes for details.

For example, the thousands of greens in the Mauritian nature are depicted beautifully with endemic plants and lush flora, and same goes for the thousands of blues that showed the marvel of our underwater life.

Credits

Vincent Montocchio, CIRCUS!, Executive Creative Director

Sharon Gouges, CIRCUS!, Creative Director

Lara Marot, CIRCUS!, Client Service Director

Diana Botte, CIRCUS!, Client Service

Romain Cotegah, CIRCUS!, Art Director

Noah Nany, CIRCUS!, Illustrator

Ravissen Pillay, CIRCUS!, 3D Artist

Blue Ramdial, Phosphore, Photographer

Mauvilac Thousands

Thousand of Mauritian Blues

BRAND Stella Artois Africa
ENTRANT COMPANY King James Group, Cape Town, South Africa
AWARD Gold

Wet Paint

Background:

South Africans experienced some of the harshest lockdown regulations in the world. When they were eventually eased, it didn't take long before the nation started slipping back to old habits.

Idea:

We collaborated with 2 renowned South African artists to create bench installations that encouraged social distancing. 8 original artworks were made and hand-painted onto benches which lived in some of the busiest public spaces in the country.

It was the first time during the pandemic that art was used to communicate a social distance messaging in public spaces.

Stella Artois Wet Paint
3003466 views · Premiered Nov 25, 2020

Results:

Over 2,300,000 Views on YouTube

84% Average Percentage Viewed

43% View Through Rate (Benchmark = 34%)

5,000,000 South Africans Reached

26 Pieces of PR Coverage in 1 Month

3:1 Earned Media Value (Benchmark = 1.5:1)

2 renowned South African Artists

8 original artworks

People's unconscious change in behaviour was captured on film

okayafrica. VISI STYLE SYNDICATE eNCA iAfrica 702 SAWUBONA expreso africa.com SAfm

Credits

Skhumbuzo Tuswa, The King James Group, Group Head Copywriter

Lauren Mitchell, The King James Group, Group Head Art Director

Graeme Jenner, The King James Group, Executive Creative Director

Anna Nashandi, The King James Group, Business Unit Director

Wayne De Lange, Silver Bullet Films, Director

Diana Keam, Silver Bullet Films, Producer

Wet Paint

Background

When lockdown restrictions were eased for the first time in South Africa, people started slipping back into old habits that put their loved ones at risk of COVID-19 infection. People had trouble adjusting to a new way of getting together and they weren't keeping a safe distance from one another. As a social experiment in social distancing, Stella Artois - a brand with a long history of bringing people together - saw an opportunity to use art to help South Africans come together safely at some of the country's busiest public spaces.

Creative Idea

As a mischievous way to help people keep their social distance while in busy public spaces like train stations, bus stops and malls, Stella Artois collaborated with artists to create original artworks that were painted right onto the middle of benches at these locations. A permanent 'Wet Paint' sign was then left there forcing people to keep their distance on either side of the bench, without even knowing they were doing it.

Strategy

The target market is made up of +/- 30 year-old professionals living in urban cities. They strive to achieve a balance between their careers and their desire to spend quality time with the people they care about. Before the pandemic, the brand was running a global campaign titled Together in The Life Artois. In keeping with the times, this changed to 'Together Apart'.

Execution

Stella Artois partnered with two renowned South African artists, Baba Tjeko and Curious Lauren to create art that encouraged social distancing. They created 8 original artworks, which were then painted onto the middle of benches at some of the busiest public spaces in the country.

Each artwork incorporated the artists' iconic styles, while including subtle cues from Stella Artois brand assets.

A high-gloss varnish was applied to the paintings, before a final touch was added - a permanent 'Wet Paint' sign with an invitation for people to sit only on either side of the painting.

Over the next few weeks, people's unconscious change in behaviour was filmed and shared on Stella Artois', as well as the artists' digital platforms as a 'social experiment in social distancing'.

Results

Campaign Film - Over 2,300,000 Views on YouTube
84% Average Percentage Viewed
43% View Through Rate (Benchmark = 34%)
5,000,000 South Africans Reached
26 Pieces of PR Coverage in 1 Month
3:1 Earned Media Value (Benchmark = 1.5:1)

Prints

BRAND   Leadway Assurance
ENTRANT COMPANY   Adeptus Advertising, Lagos, Nigeria
AWARD   Campaign Shortlist

Eze goes to school

Credits

Bamidele Ariyo, Adeptus Advertising, Creative Director

Richard Mgbeokwii, Adeptus Advertising, Art Director

Steve Abaimu, Adeptus Advertising, Copy writer

Olushola Oladimeji, Adeptus Advertising, Copy writer

Naomi Oni, Adeptus Advertising, Account Planning

Tolulope Alawode, Adeptus Advertising, Account Planning

Babatunde Alaran, Adeptus Advertising, Copy writer

Background
Create an ad that sells EPP and ESP as plans that every home in Nigeria should consider, seeing that events can happen to disrupt the successful completion of their child's education.

Creative Idea
The campaign underscores the importance of education in the life of every child as was published in the book Eze goes to school and Eze goes to college.

It further banks on the challenges faced by EZE which can be averted with a proper Education Insurance Policy. The nostalgic effect this will give to older parents was tapped into to grab attention which will spur a response to the AD call to action.

Strategy
The imperatives of securing the child's future took a nostalgic approach to ensure parents actively subscribe to either the ESP and EPP plan. This idea was targeted at parents who are working class with a consistent Income, and willing to understand the importance of Educational Insurance.

Execution
Education they say is key. This idea uses broken bricks and children looking devastated to show how dejected to see the "future" of kids crumble if not secured.

Eze goes to school

BRAND Noah's Ark Communications Limited
ENTRANT COMPANY Noah's Ark Communications Limited, Lagos, Nigeria
AWARD Campaign Bronze

Xenophobia

#SayNoToXenophobia

NOAH'S ARK

Credits

Lanre Adisa, Noah's Ark Communications Limited, Lagos, Nigeria, CCO

Bolaji Alausa, Noah's Ark Communications Limited, Lagos, Nigeria, ECD

Maurice Ugwonoh, Noah's Ark Communications Limited, Lagos, Nigeria, CD

Solomon Osafile, Noah's Ark Communications Limited, Deputy Creative Director

Adedeji Adeleke, Noah's Ark Communications Limited, Planner

Xenophobia

Background

Following the ruthless xenophobic attacks on foreign Africans who had migrated to South Africa earlier in the year, a series of events occured which seemed to drive a wedge between South Africans and the rest of Africa; as fellow Africans felt like they were being betrayed and had started to seek revenge. It is against this backdrop Noah's Ark Communications decided to run a campaign showing our stand against xenophobia.

Creative Idea

Following the insight that the xenophobia attacks was suicide in its own right, we sought to show that we (Africans) needed to stop the attacks or we we were only going to harm ourselves.

Strategy

As Africans, it is only sensible that we work and stick together for the betterment of the continent. Hence, any harm we cause to a fellow African, is basically harm to ourselves, In the wake of the xenophobic attacks, the strategy for the #SayNoToXenohobia campaign was to show that the xenophobia attacks were basically us dying by our own hands. Ergo, committing suicide.

Execution

We created various images which portrayed a person each strangling themselves to death with the South African flag as backdrop. This was followed by the copy #SayNoToXenophobia.

Results

Our results are best captured in qualitative metrics such as the talk-ability that was generated both offline and online.
From a business side of things, inquiries into what agency did this by people of interest led to new business opportunities for the agency.

Credits

Sodiq Sheu, Noah's Ark Communications Limited, Art Director

Yekeen Ibrahim, Noah's Ark Communications Limited, Art Director

Mitchelle Defounga, Noah's Ark Communications Limited, Art Director

Nike Ladokun, Noah's Ark Communications Limited, Copywriter

Dunni Elemide, Noah's Ark Communications Limited, Copywriter

Toke Mabayomije, Noah's Ark Communications Limited, Copywriter

Adeola Ogunade, Noah's Ark Communications Limited, Brand Manager

Bidemi Alfred, Noah's Ark Communications Limited, Brand Manager

Anita Erhirhie, Noah's Ark Communications Limited, Brand Manager

Patience Ugbe, Noah's Ark Communications Limited, Operations

Daniel Akintobi, Noah's Ark Communications Limited, Operations

Ife Tabi, Noah's Ark Communications Limited, Planner

Xenophobia

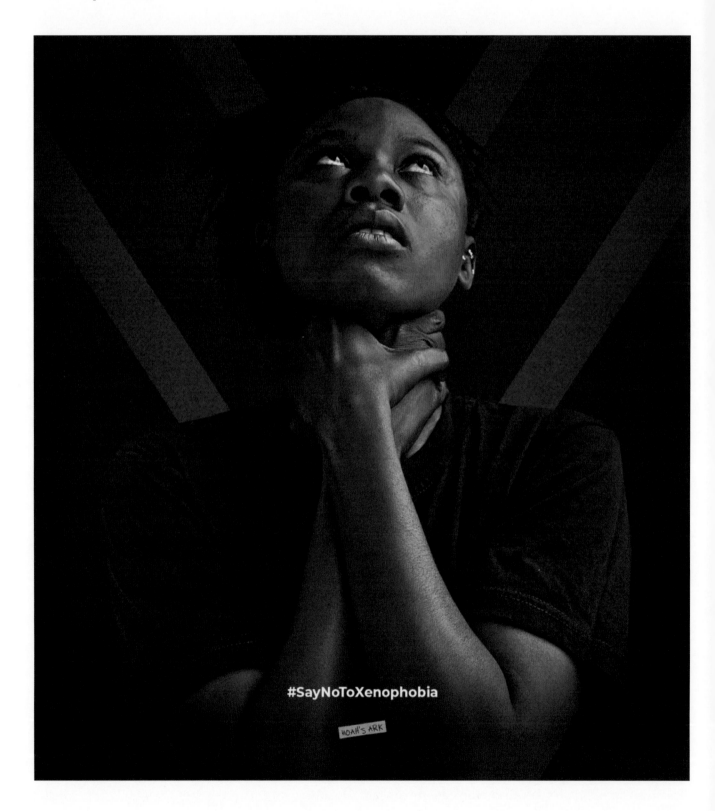

Xenophobia

BRAND   Noah's Ark Communications Limited

ENTRANT COMPANY   Noah's Ark Communications Limited, Lagos, Nigeria

AWARD   Campaign Shortlist

Noah's Ark Communications Limited (13th Anniversary)

Terrible Teens

Credits

Lanre Adisa, Noah's Ark Communications Limited, Lagos, Nigeria, CCO

Bolaji Alausa, Noah's Ark Communications Limited, Lagos, Nigeria, ECD

Maurice Ugwonoh, Noah's Ark Communications Limited, Lagos, Nigeria, CD

Solomon Osafile, Noah's Ark Communications Limited, Deputy Creative Director

Noah's Ark Communications Limited (13th Anniversary)

Background
The teenage years are years for discovery, exploration and the drive to try out new things. From our hormones acting out to the body literally trying to figure out what to do with all the new limbs and feelings, the teenage years are years we never forget in our lifetime. So why not make it a memorable one?

It is with this question ringing in the mind of the Arknimals of Noah's Ark that we decided to go all out in celebrating our 13th year anniversary and our new title as "The Latest Teenagers" in the creative industry.

Creative Idea
As excited teenagers, we wanted to show off our craziness and creativity. We took ways in which teenagers like to show off on social media as well as acts they liked to indulge in and spinned it to represent ourselves as we are determined to make these teenage years as memorable as possible.

Strategy
The challenge was, "How best can we celebrate our 13th Year Anniversary in a way that was true to form?". We decided to embrace all it means to be a Teenager. From the vices, to the mood swings and discoveries. Basically, the strategy became to show that we were willing to try out anything that came with being a teenager (With a drizzle of sanity of course!).

Execution
We created images showing some Arknimals of Noah's Ark wilding out, going crazy, enjoying trying out new things and just being Terrible teens in general.

Results
Our results are perhaps best captured not in numbers but more in qualitative metrics such as the talk-ability that was generated both offline and online.
From a business side of things, inquiries into what agency did this by people of interest led to new business opportunities for the agency.

Credits

Adedeji Adeleke, Noah's Ark Communication Limited, Planner

Jideobi Okwonkwo, Noah's Ark Communication Limited, Illustrator

Patience Ugbe, Noah's Ark Communication Limited, Operations

Daniel Akintobi, Noah's Ark Communication Limited, Operations

Ife Tabi, Noah's Ark Communication Limited, Planner

Noah's Ark Communications Limited (13th Anniversary)

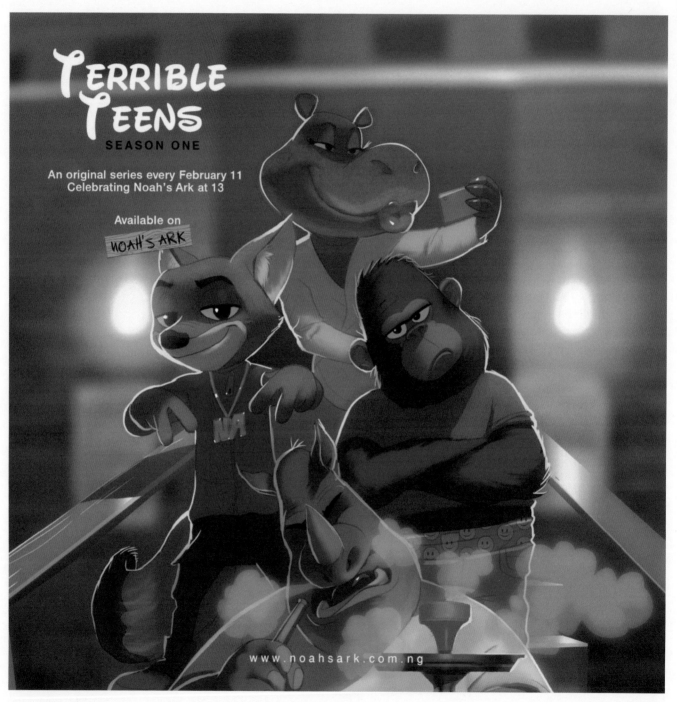

Terrible Teens

BRAND   Mauvilac Industries Ltd
ENTRANT COMPANY CIRCUS! Mauritius, Moka, Mauritius
AWARD   Campaign Bronze

Mauvilac Colourvogue 2020

Living Room

Mauvilac Colourvogue 2020

Background
Mauvilac, a local paint manufacturer in Mauritius, is used to giving a full range of its latest and most trendy and sexy colours to the public though a catalogue called Colour Vogue.

Creative Idea
The problems with catalogues is that they are never really sexy or trendy.
This year, our inspiration drove us towards an art installation using fashion and contemporary art to present the new colours. So we created a whole universe using only painting elements and tools.

Strategy
Lead like an art installation, the coulours were integrated in the whole setup to bring the colours to life. Models and sets were presented in a novel and creative way to showcase the latest trends and colours. The artworks were then filmed and stills were used on various mediums which caught the ey of the public, as well as those of the top-notch influencers, architects and interior decorators to discover Mauvilac's new range of colours.

Execution
Brushes, pots, lids and reconverted paint samples were used throughout in a creative way to create an unforgettable art installation that is inspired fashion and contemporary art.

Results
The colours were brought to life through the painted bodies of the different models who were made to look like a living masterpiece in each room of the house.

Credits

Vincent Montocchio, CIRCUS!, Executive Creative Director

Sharon Gouges Gouges, CIRCUS!, Creative Director

Melissa Veerapen, CIRCUS!, Art Director

Lara Marot, CIRCUS!, Client Service Director

Diana Botte, CIRCUS!, Client Service

Julie Telot, CIRCUS!, Designer

Danitza Vithilingem, CIRCUS!, Producer

Jean Christophe Ah Seng, CIRCUS!, Production Manager

Kunal Jankee, Freelance, Photographer

Mauvilac Colourvogue 2020

Butterfly

Mauvilac Colourvogue 2020

Terrace

BRAND   Saudabel
ENTRANT COMPANY   3Verse, Cape Town, South Africa
AWARD   Campaign Shortlist

Live Happy Side Up

Credits

Ivan Johnson, 3Verse, Executive Creative Director

Kyle Cockeran, 3Verse, Creative Director

Peni Buckton, 3Verse, Art Director

Kat Jonas, 3Verse, Art Director/Copywriter

Matt Bayly, 3Verse, Head of Art

Richard Meissenheimer, 3Verse, Finished Art

Seymour Lottering, 3Verse, Traffic/Art Buying

Live Happy Side Up

Background
Saudabel, Angola's premier water brand, was facing increased market competition, and, after 20 years as the nation's iconic water, was in need of a refresh.

Creative Idea
It's only when you turn the trademark Saudabel® water drum upside down that you get to enjoy all the fresh, wholesome, purity and vitality inside. A sight synonymous with Saudabel for more than 20 years.

Strategy
Middle to upper income Angolans, corporates and expatriates were the targets in this campaign - the idea being to refocus consumers on Saudabel's iconic status in Angola, using its trademark 5-gallon flip-barrel as the impetus for the campaign.

Execution
We took a selection of people from our typical target market and depicted them enjoying themselves in their everyday lives - but turned the shots upside down... a reference to the fact that the bottle itself has to be turned upside down in its 5-gallon dispenser unit in order to be used and enjoyed.

Results
Orders: up 62%. Spontaneous Awareness: up 24.5%. Website Traffic: up 48%.

Credits

Ray Kippie, 3Verse, Production

Joanne Stone, 3Verse, Client Service

Brittany Priest-Jones, 3Verse, Client Service

Kay Orlandi, 3Verse, Strategy

Andrew Alexander, 3Verse, Managing Partner

Sheila Stiller, Saudabel, Managing Director

Eckhard Stiller, Saudabel, Managing Partner

Claire Tanner-Roberts, 3Verse, Senior Copywriter

Live Happy Side Up

Live Happy Side Up

Live Happy Side Up

Live Happy Side Up

BRAND	Hacey Foundation
ENTRANT COMPANY	Noah's Ark Communications Limited, Lagos, Nigeria
AWARD	Campaign Gold

Stop Female Genital Mutilation

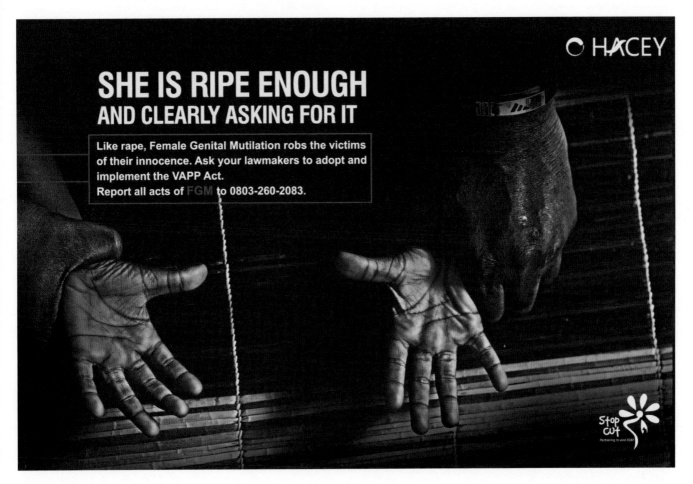

Guardian

Credits

Lanre Adisa, Noah's Ark Communications Limited, Lagos, Nigeria, CCO

Bolaji Alausa, Noah's Ark Communications Limited, Lagos, Nigeria, ECD

Ekene Eyo, Noah's Ark Communications Limited, Lagos, Nigeria, COO

Maurice Ugwonoh, Noah's Ark Communications Limited, Lagos, Nigeria, CD

Segun Odejimi, Noah's Ark Communications Limited, Lagos, Nigeria, CW

Stop Female Genital Mutilation

Background
The mutilation of the female genitals is a despicable act committed on females, not only in Nigeria, but in several other countries; both African and Non- African. With no known benefits, this act further has a snowball effect on the self-esteem, health and the life of women. Although, in Nigeria, there's a law called the VAPP Act that makes FGM a punishable act, it has not been implemented by all states and convictions via this act are few and far between. With this FGM being especially prevalent in Nigeria, with 1 out of every 10 mutilated women in the world being NIgerian, we needed to call attention to the menace that has long since gone unchecked.

It is against this backdrop, that the agency chose to develop an awareness campaign which would aid in dissuading people from committing this act.

Creative Idea
The idea was to call out the similarity between FGM and another act which always hits close to home, Rape. The idea was born out of the insight that there are other ways to rob a girl child of innocence and life's pleasures besides just rape; one of which is female genital mutilation. This was done to bring the act of FGM closer to people so that they can understand just how bad FGM is for women and how, like rape, it is an infringement of women's right and thus, is punishable by law.

Strategy
In partnership with hacey, the strategy guiding this campaign was to get people to know about the absurdity and existence of FGM in a way that would get the perpetrators to stop doing it and the bystanders to take an active stand against it .

Execution
We used a series of chilling, horror-themed visuals and stories to draw public attention to the gravity of FGM as compared to rape and child trafficking.

Prints and videos showing female body parts forcefully being held down by male hands were created. With copies calling out the similarities between the act of Rape and FGM, people were urged to also be proactive in curbing the act by lobbying their lawmakers into implementing the VAPP act and to report any acts of FGM they see being committed.

Credits

Jesujoba Popoola, Noah's Ark Communications Limited, Lagos, Nigeria, CW

Mabayomijie Akinyemi, Noah's Ark Communications Limited, Lagos, Nigeria, CW

Jumoke Akinyele, Noah's Ark Communications Limited, Lagos, Nigeria, BM

Maria Omole, Noah's Ark Communications Limited, Lagos, Nigeria, BM

Ojumi Olufade, Noah's Ark Communications Limited, Lagos, Nigeria, BM

Patience Ugbe, Noah's Ark Communications Limited, Lagos, Nigeria, Operations

Stop Female Genital Mutilation

Father

Stop Female Genital Mutilation

Mother

Stop Female Genital Mutilation

Sister

MEDIA AGENCY
OF THE YEAR

mediaReach OMD Lagos, Nigeria

ADVERTISING AGENCY
OF THE YEAR

King James Group, Cape Town, South Africa

KINGJAMES GROUP **SA**

Pitcher
FESTIVAL OF CREATIVITY

Celebrating Outstanding Creativity in Africa

PROGRAMMES INCLUDE:

FUTURE CREATIVE LEADERS ACADEMY

This is an intensive 3-day professional immersion programme for students in tertiary institutions. It is supported by the Advertising Practitioners Council of Nigeria (APCON). The Academy annually recognizes the best participating universities, lecturers and students. Winners in the FCLA competitions are sponsored to attend the Roger Hatchuel Academy in Cannes and the Dubai Lynx.

YOUNG PROFESSIONALS ACADEMY

The Young Professionals Academy is a bespoke learning programme for creative communications professionals of up to 30 years. In addition to the intensive learning opportunities, participants also engage in highly rewarding competitions like the Young Lions Competitions, where winners have the chance to represent their country in Cannes and the Young Pitcher Integrated Competition, where winners are sponsored to attend the Dubai Lynx.

CREATING A BETTER AFRICA

The Creating a Better Africa(CBA) Sustainability Programme is a high-profile career acceleration initiative for mid to senior level communications professionals. It is designed to inspire social purpose and sustainability as well as promote creativity as a catalyst for national development.

SEE IT BE IT AFRICA

See It Be It Africa is an extension of the Cannes Lions See It Be It initiative that addresses gender imbalance in creative leadership. The See It Be It Africa programme brings the message closer to more women in Africa.

PITCHER AWARDS

The Pitcher Awards celebrate outstanding work created or implemented in Africa across several categories including film, print, digital, media and PR.

PITCHER TALKS & WORKSHOPS

Pitcher Talks & Workshops present unique platforms for leading industry professionals to deliver top-notch seminars and conduct hands-on workshop sessions that focus on critical issues affecting the industry especially as it pertains to Africa.

Pitcher Festival of Creativity is organized by CHINI Africa, Cannes Lions official Festival Representative in Nigeria. For sponsorship, partnership or participation details, please send email to info@pitcherfestival.com

LEARN THE
A - Z OF WORD
JUGGLING AT OUR
COPYWRITING
CLASS

CULTURECODE
The virtual creativity school

www.culturecode.courses